THE <u>NEW</u> SELF HELP SERIES

ANGINA

Relief from the misery of angina using
relaxation techniques, exercise, diet and
alternative medicine.

THE <u>NEW</u> SELF HELP SERIES

ANGINA

ROGER NEWMAN TURNER
N.D., D.O., B.Ac., M.B.N.O.A.

THORSONS PUBLISHING GROUP

First published 1987

© R. Newman Turner 1987

For Max
who sacrificed many walks
to make this book possible.

British Library Cataloguing in Publication Data

Newman Turner, R.
New self-help for angina.
1. Angina pectoris — Treatment
2. Self-care. Health
I. Title
616.1'2206   RC685.A6

ISBN 0-7225-1301-1

*Published by Thorsons Publishers Limited,
Wellingborough, Northamptonshire, NN8 2RQ,
England.*

Printed in Great Britain by Richard Clay Limited,
Bungay, Suffolk.

3 5 7 9 10 8 6 4

Contents

		Page
Acknowledgements		7
Introduction		9
Chapter		
1.	Understanding Angina	15
2.	Lifestyle and Angina	32
3.	Learning to Cope	45
4.	Rest and Exercise	57
5.	Food and Drink	80
6.	Seeking Professional Help	107
Further Reading		120
Useful Addresses		122
Index		126

Acknowledgements

The development of a method of management for any condition which afflicts mankind calls for a variety of skills and a broad area of experience. In preparing this guide for the patient with angina I have drawn upon the expertise of people in many fields of health care. I hope, in particular, that I have absorbed sufficient of the wisdom of my colleagues in the naturopathic, osteopathic, and acupuncture professions to pass on to the reader.

One of the pioneers in the field of humanistic cardiology, and the founder of a society for the promotion of these aims, is Dr Peter Nixon to whom I am indebted for much valuable information and source material. Dr Nixon's caring and innovative team at the Cardiology Department of Charing Cross Hospital, London, includes the Occupational Therapists, led by Miss Jenny King, who has also been most helpful.

Once again my deepest gratitude is due to Mrs Lynne Metcalfe, who has shown a determined dedication to the preparation of the manuscript, and to my wife and family, who have remained loyal and loving through many months of neglect.

Roger Newman Turner
Letchworth, 1986

Introduction

You are probably reading this because you have angina, or, possibly, someone close to you has angina. The onset of angina not only strikes a devastating blow to its victims, but also impinges upon the lives of those around them.

Angina induces apprehension, anxiety, and fear. It curtails physical activity and leads to a loss of self-esteem. A feeling of helplessness prevails which is fuelled by ignorance about the condition and confusion about the various theories as to its causes.

Yet, angina is only a symptom, a warning that all is not well in the economy of the body and, if acted upon constructively, can mark the start of a healthier, more evenly paced life. The concern over angina is that much greater because it signals trouble with the heart. Certainly the heart may be failing to cope with the demands made upon it. This can be due partly to changes in the coronary arteries which carry blood to the heart muscles, but the real disease may be the exhaustion of the mind and the depletion of physical reserves which have led to the point of breakdown marked by the onset of the symptoms.

This raises other issues which need considering. How fit is the heart to cope with its demands? Are these demands too great for its present state of fitness? Is it adequately nourished, rested, and well-trained?

Of course, all these are concerns not just for the heart but for the whole body and it is to the attainment of better health at all levels, nutritional, structural, psychological, and spiritual, that the guidance in this book is directed. It is based on the most up-to-date scientific and clinical knowledge derived from the study of heart-related diseases and nutritional biochemistry as well as that in the fields of relaxation and meditation. By its application the angina sufferer places himself in a position of greater strength and has more positive strategies with which to cope with the disorder.

This is not to suggest that expert medical attention will not continue to be necessary. The heart and blood-pressure must continue to be monitored and the management of the pain-controlling drugs may still be required, but, by taking some personal responsibility for his health, the angina sufferer can get away from the mentality in which he sees himself as a helpless victim of irreversible mechanical changes. The new knowledge gained by research in nutrition, exercise, and stress management has shown that angina is both preventable and controllable by personal effort, and that the enormous toll of degenerative heart-disease could be dramatically reduced if more people were to play an active part in caring for themselves. There is more and more evidence that the adoption of a healthier life-style and avoiding excessive stress can reduce the tremendous toll of heart-disease and the enormously costly medical interventions which are popular at present.

Heart-disease is a major scourge of the developed countries and it is the biggest cause of death in many of them including the UK, where, according to Professor John Catford, Director of Heartbeat Wales, a health education project, the numbers who die from heart attacks and strokes is equivalent to a jumbo jet crashing every day. Many of these are sudden deaths with little or no previous warning. Many more are lucky enough to have the alarm system triggered in the form of angina and, if they heed it and take effective action, they have a good prospect of restoring reasonable health.

The Mechanical View

The prevailing medical view sees angina as a mechanical problem, due primarily to narrowing of the coronary arteries. The progressive restriction of blood flow deprives the walls of the ventricles, the major chambers of the heart, of oxygen and they are unable to meet the extra demands made upon them during exercise. As the pressure builds up in the ventricles pain is referred, via the spinal cord, to the chest, neck, and arms.

Management consists of the use of drugs, such as glyceryl trinitrate, which relieves attacks by dilating the blood vessels and reducing the ventricular pressure. Other drugs may be prescribed to reduce blood-pressure and a group known as beta-blockers, are now widely used to reduce nerve impulses so that the heart, and other muscles, do not respond so vigorously to general arousal.

All these drugs are tried and tested and found very effective at what they were designed for. They are, indeed, essential in some cases but they have two big drawbacks. They do not deal with the real causes of angina, and they have side-effects which include putting the heart itself at further disadvantage.

A mechanical view of disease inevitably leads to a mechanical treatment and it is not surprising that one of the most widely used approaches to coronary artery disease is the by-pass operation. In America over 100,000 coronary by-pass operations are performed every year and 60% of heart surgical cases in the UK are for coronary vessel disease. The results are impressive; 90% improve after surgery and at least 75% become completely free of symptoms. But is the relief or removal of symptoms all there is to the management of angina? Do all those who successfully undergo surgery manage to make an effective return to normal work? The evidence seems to suggest that they do not.

Drugs and surgery are pretty radical approaches but doctors are on the whole very conservative about the introduction of new ideas and seem particularly reluctant to intrude in any way on the patient's lifestyle. Yet the majority of people with angina would be only too glad to take some steps to help themselves.

The information now available to us about the role of nutrition, exercise, and stress in the cause of angina provides many ways of coping with it which are non-invasive and constructive. Some of them are the subject of much debate and controversy, and the advantages are not as clearly defined as those of drugs and surgery, which may partly account for their slow acceptance.

How much exercise is correct? Should fats be reduced? Does smoking really make any difference? What is the role of sugar? The relevance of these issues will be different for each case but there is enough evidence on all of them to be worth looking at. Diet, exercise, and attitudes are all controllable factors which can affect the quality of the life of the angina patient and it is, therefore, worth incorporating some action on all fronts towards improving these. There is nothing to lose, and possibly a great deal to gain.

1.

Understanding Angina

One of the most unpleasant aspects of any pain or illness is not knowing what is happening to you. Uncertainty invariably fans the flames of anxiety to a height quite disproportionate to the severity of the complaint or, alternatively, chills one into a dangerous indifference to symptoms that may herald a need for sensible and timely intervention.

With angina the anxiety is compounded by the knowledge that the heart may be involved and that implies a threat to life itself. From the earliest times the heart has held vital significance. The Chinese regarded it as the seat of the spirit for almost two millenia before William Harvey described its function as a circulatory pump.

Oddly enough, the severe discomfort of angina is not that of the heart itself since it has no nerves which register pain. It is the consequence of its inability to cope with its physical demands of which the angina patient becomes aware. The overworked heart becomes distended and as pressure rises in the left ventricle, the main pump to the whole body, pulsations are set up which refer pain, via the spinal cord, to the chest, neck, and arms. This is why it is important to differentiate true angina, which originates in the heart, from pains due to other causes such as indigestion, fibrositis, intercostal neuritis, and restrictions of bones in the neck and upper back. Because they all bear a vague resemblance to angina, but do not originate in the heart, they are known as false angina or pseudo-angina.

True angina is distinguished by the gripping severity of the pain, which may occur at any time, but is usually associated with effort or stress — hurrying to catch a train to work, for example. The pain may last for as little as thirty seconds but can persist for up to thirty minutes. The diagnosis is generally confirmed if it is relieved by the drug glyceryl trinitrate, which dilates the blood vessels and relieves the pressure in the left ventricle. This gives rapid relief but the short-term effects should not become a substitute for long-term management of the real causes of angina.

Coronary Arteries

The major source of the trouble is believed to be the coronary arteries, the three vessels which carry blood to the muscle walls of the heart (Figure 1). The efficiency with which they do this is critical to its healthy function as the main pump in our circulatory system. If the coronary arteries become narrowed or obstructed the amount of oxygen-carrying blood reaching the heart muscles will diminish and they become less effective in performing their contractions.

This leads to the overloading of the ventricles and the pain of angina.

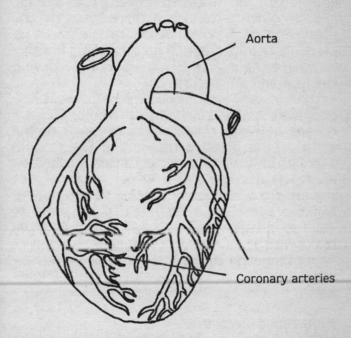

Figure 1:   The coronary arteries

If the obstruction to the flow of blood through one or more of the coronary arteries is particularly severe the muscle fibres supplied by those vessels will atrophy. The muscles, deprived of oxygen, will simply cease to function and the individual will have a heart attack, the severity of which will depend on how big an area of heart muscle is affected. When a large area is involved, possibly because of blockage of the main coronary artery, the heart attack will be fatal. Many people with angina may have already had a heart attack of varying severity and be well on the road to recovery, but for anyone with the condition there is always the possibility of further deterioration, so it is particularly important to do something positive to reduce the risk rather than simply relieving the pain when it occurs.

The coronary arteries become narrow because of damage to the linings by atheroma. This is a deposit of fatty material which clings to the walls of the arteries rather like the calcium deposits in a water pipe. It causes a condition known as atherosclerosis. As particular parts of the arterial wall become thickened the flow of blood is altered and further deposits tend to build up in the same way as silt accumulates on the bend in a river. Occasionally fragments break away and these, if sufficiently large, may block a branch of the coronary arteries (Figure 2).

High Blood-Pressure

Various factors contribute to the development of atheroma, many of them preventable. High blood-pressure is a major risk factor because the extra pressure on the circulatory system forces fatty material through the damaged linings into the arterial wall. For this to happen the active fats must be present in excess. We all need some fats to carry vitamins and help make essential hormones but when they get too thick in the blood they are liable to form deposits. We can control these fatty deposits by dietary management and with the aid of certain herbs and supplements.

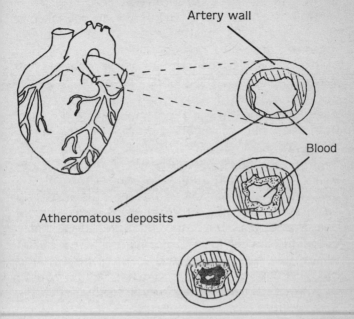

Figure 2:   Fatty deposits (atheroma) gradually build
            up in the coronary arteries

Sticky Platelets

The blood platelets can also cause trouble when
they become too adhesive. The platelets are
special cells which clump together to form a
protective mesh which seals wounds when we
are cut, but if they become too sticky the blood
may clot more readily in the vessels where it is
inappropriate to do so.

These clotted particles can block narrowed or
obstructed arteries which may give rise to
anginal pain or heart attacks.

Stimulants, Sloth, and Stress

It isn't just food and drink which affect our blood fats and the stickiness of our platelets. Cigarette smoking, obesity, lack of exercise, and stress may also contribute to a rise of the saturated fats in the blood. The ways in which obesity and slothfulness may result in a rise in levels of blood fats are, perhaps, fairly obvious, but the role of cigarettes may seem more puzzling.

Smoking increases the levels of noradrenalin, a hormone which maintains the tone of the circulation and nervous system. This is partly why cigarettes give a temporary feeling of well-being and can become addictive. Constantly sustained levels of noradrenalin and adrenalin will, however, reduce our oxygen levels and increase carbon dioxide and other fatigue waste products which may eventually initiate atherosclerosis.

One of the most potent causes of increased adrenalin and noradrenalin output is stress. Stress is normal and necessary to our creative drive; it is what has enabled us to survive as a species — having to adapt to our changing environment. But sustained stress with regularly high levels of noradrenalin and adrenalin, collectively known as the catecholamines or destructive hormones, will have the damaging effects already described before eventual fatigue sets in. Some people's lifestyle keeps them in a high level of arousal for years — often laying down deposits and fatiguing the heart until it can no longer cope.

Other stimulants such as coffee, owing to its

caffeine content, may also sustain a high level of arousal. Several other beverages, such as cola drinks, contain high levels of caffeine which make them unsuitable for the angina case. Even small amounts of caffeine cause increased excitability of the nervous system. This may, for a while, counter mental fatigue, but there is often inadequate nourishment to sustain the increased activity. As a consequence coffee, or any other caffeine-containing drink, compounds the exhaustion. In spite of the fact that the pharmacological effect of caffeine is to dilate the coronary arteries people with angina often find that it induces or aggravates their symptoms. This is probably because it increases the heart rate and makes the ventricular pressure rise.

It is evident that a fatty furring up of the coronary arteries may not be the only cause of angina. Many patients who experience chest pain can have normal arteries, including up to 15% of those referred for by-pass surgery. When we also consider that some authorities report little objective improvement, and a poor rate of return to normal work, after by-pass surgery amongst a particular group of patients studied, it does question the validity of the procedure when carried out without proper guidance and management of the real causes of the disturbance — overwork and fatigue coupled with unreasonable stress — which put an intolerable burden on the physically unfit heart.

The figures for return to work after surgery are high because in the USA there are greater financial pressures to start earning. But they do not indicate the long-term progress or efficiency of those returning to employment, nor can they reflect the loss of self-regard and psychological trauma which occurs after surgery. There is a real need for alternative strategies in the management of angina.

IDENTIFYING ANGINA

If you start getting chest pains the first thing you need to do is to ascertain the cause. Angina pains are quite distinctive but there are a number of other reasons for chest pain which can be misleading and may be sources of great anxiety.

The pain of angina is usually rather sudden in onset and can be quite severe. There is a feeling of oppression around the heart and the pain radiates to the left shoulder and arm, most commonly, but can also go the neck or jaw on either side, the centre of the back, or to the abdomen. It all depends which nerve pathways the constricting messages from the heart decide to take. Once irritating impulses reach the spinal cord they can jump up or down to different segments which transmit reflex messages to various unrelated areas (Figure 3).

One of the most striking features of angina is the way that it can occur during spells of effort and exertion bringing the victim to a standstill for a time — what one expert describes as "the imperious arrest of angina". After a short rest he may be able to carry on, only soon to be halted again. The frustrating, but distinctive symptom of angina-of-effort is that the pain may occur only occasionally when walking, so the sufferer needs to slow down or stop, and this may occur regardless of the distance which can be walked at other times. This can give us some further insight into the management of angina.

An interesting example was L.A., a 53 year-old insurance executive, who noticed that his angina attacks would occur when he was walking to the station but, only, as a rule, when he was on his way to work. When he was just going for a day out they didn't come on. The

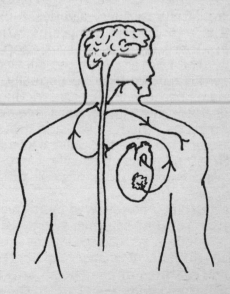

Figure 3: Pain messages from the heart travel via the spinal cord to the jaw, chest, or left arm

whole concept of effort is absolutely crucial to our understanding of angina and we shall look more closely at this later.

It isn't only physical exertion which induces attacks. One lady, a retired administrator aged 70, described how a pain, like indigestion, would come on in the night, move up to the jaws, and cause a tingling of the fingers.

Angina of Coronary Thrombosis

Sometimes the pains which come on without effort are of greater intensity. They are usually associated with angina of coronary thrombosis, the type which is caused by blocking or narrowing of the coronary arteries.

There are, of course, symptoms other than the pain. There is occasionally a shortness of breath — the restriction of the chest muscles makes it difficult to breathe normally. Angina got its name because of this constricting effect. It comes from the Greek word *angere* which means to choke. The face will also become pale with perspiration, and the pulse becomes more rapid. The blood-pressure usually rises during an attack. These are all signs of crisis or shock in the body.

The attack may be followed by flatulence and an increased output of urine, two more factors which are often associated with the body's response to fear. Perhaps one of the most disturbing features of the angina attack is the sense of foreboding or doom which the sufferer describes. The symptoms of angina bring us back repeatedly to the strong emotional and psychological impact of the condition.

Pseudo-Angina

There are a number of disorders which can mimic the pain of angina quite alarmingly, not least an acute anxiety state itself. The colloquialism 'uptight' describes the situation well. There is a surge of energy and blood up to the head, the brain works overtime, and the muscles of the neck, shoulders, and back become tight and fixed.

Tense muscles in the middle of the back between the shoulders can lock up the bones in the spinal column. When these lose their normal freedom of movement the whole chest can become restricted because the ribs are attached, like bucket handles, to the vertebrae at the back and to the sternum at the front. Spasm of the muscles, or fixation of several of the vertebrae between the shoulder blades, can cause constrictions and pain in the chest.

To add to the confusion this can occur when carrying out physical activities, especially those which involve the arms and shoulders, such as painting or papering a ceiling. Chest pain from musculo-skeletal causes can also come on in bed because tense muscle fibres do not relax fully at rest so become stiffer when there isn't much movement to stretch them and stimulate the circulation. Usually moving about a bit and rolling the shoulders will loosen things up.

Hyperventilation

A further consequence of anxiety is a tendency to breathe more rapidly and for the respiration to become more shallow. This hyperventilation results in a disturbance of the ratio of oxygen to carbon-dioxide in the blood which may cause angina-like pains. The hyperventilation syndrome can be overcome by teaching the individual correct breathing with long outward breaths.

Indigestion is often a cause of chest discomfort. A distended stomach may even embarrass the heart by putting some pressure on it through the diaphragm. Other digestive disorders, if chronic, may cause a negative feedback to the nerves which originate in the spinal cord at the level of the shoulder blades leading to the sort of nervous restrictions described above. This is known as a viscero-somatic reflex because messages from the viscera (stomach, intestines, and so on) are transmitted to the body surface (soma) (see Figure 3). They can also work the other way. Long-standing restrictions of muscles or joints in the neck or upper back may cause prolonged irritation of the nerves which supply vital organs, such as the heart and stomach. We shall look more closely at the influence of body posture and exercise in Chapter 4.

Although the heart is not directly responsible for these pains paradoxically their causes can also contribute to, or aggravate, true angina. Angina-of-effort can be brought on more readily after a heavy meal; the somatico-visceral reflex can operate, the restrictions of the spine contributing to the constriction of the coronary arteries; and over-aroused emotions can seize up not only the mind but also the heart muscles.

Getting a Check-Up

So, if you experience any recurring or persistent pains, it would be wise to seek medical advice to determine whether or not the heart is really involved. Your doctor, or a natural therapy practitioner, will be able to determine a certain amount from a physical examination, which includes checking the pulse and blood-pressure, but they will also need to have tests done to measure the amount of cholesterol and total fats in your blood. High levels of these would suggest a susceptibility to atherosclerosis which might be reinforced by signs visible in the retina of the eyes as well as some other parts of the body.

The blood can also be tested for the presence of certain enzymes which may be evident for several days after damage to the heart muscles. If there has been a mild heart attack, for example, the oxygen-deprived muscles in the walls of the ventricles will release these enzymes.

Heart efficiency can also be checked by simple exercise-tolerance tests. One of the reasons angina develops is because the heart becomes fatigued and fails to meet the demands which are made upon it. It is simply not fit enough and like any other muscles, if it doesn't get an adequate balance of rest and exercise it will start to decline in vitality.

The exercise-tolerance test is a simple matter of measuring the changes in pulse rate after stepping on and off a low stool or platform for one minute. The pulse rate will, of course, increase initially but after a rest of three minutes should return to almost normal. In some clinics and hospitals they use a treadmill test in which the heart and the blood-pressure can be monitored while the individual exercises on a moving belt. The only drawback of this method is that, for some patients, the array of technology which surrounds such tests causes added anxiety which adversely affects the results.

Personality and Angina

Of course it must be remembered that it is not simply hearts and arteries that get angina, it is people. It is now possible to predict who will be more susceptible to heart disease not only on the basis of dietary habits, lack of exercise, or heavy smoking, but also by assessing the personality. Clinics specializing in coronary disease prevention use questionnaires to determine whether there is a high degree of competitiveness and aggression, the characteristics which make an individual more prone to heart-disease and angina.

We tend to equate the overweight, rich-living, cigarette-smoking, under-exercised, thickset, executive male as the person who gets angina, but it strikes right across the social and physical scale. The slight of build, mild-mannered person is just as likely to be a victim, particularly if subjected to the frustrations and monotony of unsatisfactory work.

Although true angina is ten times as common in men as in women, the latter can still suffer quite severe pains. They are, however, more prone to pseudo-angina. Men bottle up their emotions much more than women and this internalization of aggression may inflict more damaging effects on the heart and arteries of the male.

Hereditary Factors

There is a strong tendency for heart disease to run in families. We all inherit a certain degree of 'organ inferiority' in much the same way as we inherit features of face or feet. An essential part of our unique individuality is determined by our genetic make up. This may endow us with less efficient hearts or livers, or with subtle susceptibilities of body chemistry which allow us to accumulate too much cholesterol. There is, for example, a condition known as familial hypercholesterolaemia, in which the males of a family tend to produce excessive amounts of cholesterol. Fortunately, hereditary trends are seldom so bad that disease is inevitable. We all have the capacity to adapt our diet and lifestyle in such a way as to minimize the risk of the weak links in our genetic chain giving way.

Taking Control

Clearly there are many factors which influence your susceptibility to angina. Some of them, like hereditary tendencies, are partially beyond your control. Once degenerative changes have occurred in the heart and the arteries they can sometimes be reversed and the heart can be retrained, but there may be some limitations which you have to accept.

Perhaps there are even aspects of your personality, or situations in your work or social life which cannot easily be altered. But there are so many factors which are controllable, a number of which can significantly affect the way you cope with the ones you can't change, that it is worth exploring them more fully.

The confusing thing for the angina sufferer is the debate over what factors are most important in the management of heart-disease. There are experts who say that diet is the most important influence and others who say it is not, and amongst those who do there is still disagreement as to whether fats, carbohydrates or salt are the most important risk factors. Then there are people who believe that exercise is the answer, and still others who maintain that the pressures of modern life are the main cause of disease and that the cool laid-back lifestyle should be our ultimate aim.

There is no single cause of angina and no simple answer — least of all drugs or surgery. There is convincing evidence for the influence of all the risk factors in one way or another. Their relative importance may vary from person to person. For some cases the ravages of an over-rich diet may have furred up the arteries; for others the increasing demands of a highly competitive job. But it is far more likely that in most cases these danger patterns are working together to increase the 'total lesion' load — the cumulative effect of the damaging factors to health which the body has to bear.

Each individual has a reserve of adaptibility. You may give up smoking or take more exercise, and these will undoubtedly reduce the load on the negative side of the scale, but if you go on consuming large amounts of fats and sugars or chasing impossible goals in business, you are really not giving your body all the help it deserves.

You owe it the best so try and work at every level over which you have control — you can adjust your diet, you can take more rest, and you may even reduce the pressures of business. All the evidence suggests that the greatest potential for health lies in the judicious application of every resource available to you.

2.

Lifestyle and Angina

The cases described in Chapter 1 revealed some consistent clues as to the major influences on their condition and outstanding among these was the frequency with which the pain was associated with times of anxiety and rush. It is probably no coincidence that in an age when it is fashionable to be in a hurry, there is a greater incidence of angina pectoris.

It isn't only changes in our consumption of fats and sugars, or the amount of exercise we take, which can be held responsible for the higher rates of heart-disease. Our eating patterns have been fairly consistent for many years, apart from the periods of national austerity surrounding the world wars.

The significant phenomenon of the late twentieth century, at least in the developed countries, where heart-disease is most prevalent, is 'hype' — the exaggeration of trivia. Our visual and auditory senses are subjected to a constant barrage of information presented in a way calculated to excite our sense of urgency. The immediacy of the media means that every minor local upheaval is presented as an event of major national or international importance. From an early age we are wound up by the meaningless babble of pop radio and the strident beat of its constant fare, or our senses are over stimulated by the sensationalism of the popular press. It is hard for anyone moving in the mainstream of life to escape the perpetual momentum of arousal.

And yet our lifestyle is not entirely thrust upon us. It is created by our attitudes and ambitions, moulded to the social course we pursue. If that is one of creative fulfilment there should be no problem but, if our life has become desk-bound and stress-bound, there is a danger of being ground down to the crumbling point of failure to cope and, commonly, that inadequacy will express itself through the heart.

Work Pressures

Once it comes, angina affects almost every aspect of life. It cuts down the capacity for productive work, it limits the variety of vigorous, active recreation which can be undertaken, and it impairs the intellectual capacity, supplanting it with a diminished sense of self-esteem. The feelings of inadequacy physically, creatively, and emotionally, become an intolerable yoke to bear on top of the pain and anxiety of the condition itself. The restraints imposed by the physical limitations of the heart emphasize still further the sense of defeat which is often the pre-anginal predicament.

Frustration and a sense of failure are frequent precursors to the anginal syndrome and can be as damaging to the worker on the factory floor, facing the monotonous routine of a dead-end job, as to the company director, overwhelmed by the burdens of responsibility or the challenge of a difficult market and the restraints of a financial crisis. Each may feel that he should be capable of more creative or effective work but be in no position to achieve his potential.

Then there is the person who sets himself impossible targets and drives himself to the point of exhaustion trying to achieve them. The feelings of failure compound the adverse effects of the fatigue. If he were to redefine his goals to a more realistic level, a little less effort might prove more rewarding with the body appreciating the generally lower levels of adrenalin and cortisol, the catabolic or destructive hormones which tend to raise the blood-pressure and the tension in the left ventricle of the heart.

Good and Bad Stress

The high level of striving can be forced upon one by external circumstances or people, or may be self-imposed. Either way these excessive demands have come to be regarded as stress, but stress is not altogether a bad thing. Our bodies have been evolved to cope with stress. We have adapted mechanisms by which we respond to the external stimuli thrust upon us. It is these mechanisms that have enabled us to evolve over many thousands of years as our environment has changed.

Reasonable stress is the spur to our creative abilities and efficient physical performance. It is when stress becomes strain that it starts to be harmful; when the demands of our environment (climate, food, etc.), or our ambitions and responsibilities (workload, deadlines, personal anxieties) outstrip our physical and mental capacity to respond effectively.

Human Function Curve

While the body is in good physical condition and the mind well nourished, alert, and productive, reasonable effort results in adequate performance and progress with the challenges of life. In normal health, the greater the effort the higher the level of performance. But when more effort becomes necessary to maintain the same output a point may come where exhaustion overtakes effective performance and deterioration sets in.

This pattern is clearly illustrated in the Human Function Curve (Figure 4) described in *The Practitioner* (No. 217 1976) by Dr Peter Nixon FRCP, Senior Consultant Cardiologist at London's Charing Cross Hospital. The curve shows the increase of performance resulting from increased arousal or effort. Healthy tension sustains the anabolic phase of activity. When fatigue sets in declining function and destructive (catabolic) changes in the body lead, sooner or later, to the point of collapse (P).

The warning signs are an increasing physical and mental weariness with declining efficiency resulting in more 'things going wrong'. The 'slings and arrows' of life seem to increase, whether because of circumstance or one's diminishing competence matters little. A vicious

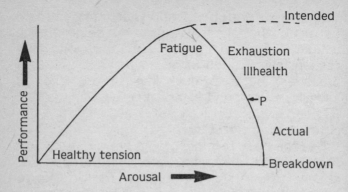

Figure 4: The Human Function Curve. Fighting on through fatigue will lead to ill health and a point of breakdown (P)

(Reproduced by kind permission of Dr P.G.F. Nixon)

circle is established in which the interplay of both physical and mental processes affects life at every level.

The loss of self esteem which follows the breakdown of health can become as destructive as the physical deterioration. Feelings of anxiety and guilt at not fulfilling one's role in the family and in society may disturb sleep and lead to more exhaustion which weakens performance still further. A destructive cycle is set up:

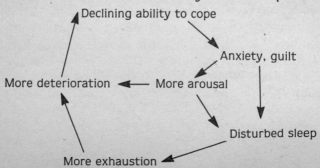

Trapped in this cycle the individual becomes less fit and, therefore, unable to cope with the sudden physical or mental demands which may be made upon him, whether they be self-imposed bursts of exercise (in an effort to get fit), or the mental pressures of added professional and personal responsibilities.

Personality Types

Not everyone falls victim to this sequence of events. Some individuals cope better, repulsing with impunity pressures which are rapidly defeating others. The ability to cope is dependent on a variety of factors determined by heredity, nutritional habits and personality.

A well-known classification of personality types was made by Drs M. Friedman and R. Rosenbaum. They described as the **Type A** personality the individual who is readily aroused to aggression, anger, hostility, haste, and impatience. Such a person is always in a hurry — the man with his hand on the hooter in a traffic jam — strives to be busy when he doesn't need to be, and is highly competitive both in work and in play.

This type is often a workaholic, having little time for leisure, but, when he does engage in recreational activities, the strongly competitive element is carried through as an excessive desire to win. This will be the person whose twice-weekly squash game becomes a blaze of belting and flying perspiration, or the one who pounds the pavements in the addictive pursuit of an even better time round the jogging route.

Type Bs are more easy going. The problems of

life and pressures of time may still assault them but they can shrug them off without becoming too worked up. They appear to have an imperviousness which protects them against the ravages of anger and aggression. They are more inclined to play for the sake of the game than to win it.

A modicum of each personality type would provide a healthy balance of creative drive with the capacity to back off when pressures become too great, but the strongly Type A individual is inclined to push through his limits to the point of exhaustion and breakdown and is more susceptible to heart attacks and angina.

Treadmill of Effort

Even though they may show a greater tendency to angina it is not a condition confined to the aggressive, ambitious, high-pressure personality. The passive quiet ones can also fall victim if their life becomes a relentless plod leading them to fatigue, aggravated by the frustration of monotony. They may have become trapped in what Dr Peter Nixon calls the Treadmill of Effort.

The humdrum routine of an unchallenging job or the irksome tie of caring for an elderly or infirm relative can still result in an unacceptably high output of destructive hormones by the release of adrenal stimulating chemicals in the brain. The cumulative effect of these undischarged tension hormones results in spasm of the arteries as well as increased blood-pressure, heart rate, blood fats, and sugar. For this type of person the best way of discharging the destructive head of steam which they build up might be to 'blow their top' occasionally. A good outburst of anger, or, better still, some form of physical discharge in pleasurable exercise, can have a therapeutic effect. But if exercise merely adds to a state of exhaustion it serves no useful purpose.

It is first necessary to replenish your reserves and, perhaps, review the circumstances of your life which may have brought you to the present predicament.

Scoring Life's Changes

Most people remain comfortable and reasonably healthy while their life follows a well-trodden path. It is the major changes, not all of them unpleasant, which present a challenge which may be met with varying degrees of adaptability. Writing in the *Journal of Psychosomatic Medicine* in 1967, T.H. Holmes and R.H. Rahe proposed a scoring system for assessing the impact of life's major upheavals. The greater the changes the higher the score. Using marriage as a yardstick they allocated it 50 points and from this scaled other events which could disturb the smooth course of life:

POINTS
100	death of a spouse
73	divorce
60–69	marital separation, imprisonment, death of a close relative
50–59	personal injury or illness
50	marriage
40–49	loss of job, marital reconciliation,

retirement, change in health of a family member, pregnancy

30–39   sex difficulties, new family member, business readjustment, change in financial condition, death of a close friend, change to a different line of work, change in number of arguments with spouse, large mortgage

20–29   foreclosure of mortgage or loan, change in responsibilities at work, son or daughter leaving home, trouble with in-laws, outstanding personal achievement, spouse begins or stops work, change in living conditions, revision of personal habits, trouble with boss, change in work hours or conditions, change in residence

10–19   changes in recreation, church or school activities, small mortgage, minor violation of law, change in eating/sleeping habits, and number of family get-togethers, vacation, Christmas

The individual's response to any of these events will depend very much on their physical fitness, nutritional status, and emotional resilience, but it is a commonly observed fact that peoples' health gives way at, or shortly after, a time of increased financial responsibility, bereavement, and so on. The vulnerable back will often give way or the immune system become less competent at such times. Consistently high scores for a period of 2 or 3 years or more will predispose towards heart-disease.

Environment

Adding to the total burdens we have to bear through life may be some over which we have little control. Among these are the environmental factors such as climate, pollution, noise, and overcrowding.

The angina sufferer always finds it harder to cope in cold weather. More effort is required to keep warm and penetrating winds stiffen the muscles and make exercise more arduous. Heat waves can also be difficult for people with heart problems. Chemicals in air and food may impair digestive efficiency thus undermining the nourishment of body and mind.

Intolerable and relentless noise, either at work or in and around the home can increase the level of arousal. The same type of physiological response is induced by the need to endure unpleasant people from whom one cannot escape or unacceptable situations over which one has no control. When it is faced with an enemy the primitive instinct of the body is to fight or run away. In work, and most social situations, one cannot do that, so the hormones which tone muscles and increase heart rate and blood-pressure just go on accumulating without discharge. The bosses of one Japanese factory recognized the importance of avoiding resentment amongst their workforce. They installed punchbag effigies of themselves in the factory gymnasium on which their employees could work off their feelings!

The Purpose of Illness

In your process of self-appraisal it is sometimes worth asking yourself what meaning lies behind your angina. What is your body trying to tell you? It is probably saying 'I can't cope with the type of life that you're leading. Please stop before I do!'

The onset of symptoms, such as angina, will often start long after the body has started to go into decline. Most bodies have remarkable reserves and will put up with a great deal before they start to complain. When they do it is wise to heed the warnings. Organic changes and patterns of dysfunction are usually quite well established by the time you become consciously aware of them. Timely action may not only arrest deterioration but, for many, has marked a real turning point in their lives.

An arresting ailment, such as angina, or a heart attack, has often been the catalyst to a process of self-evaluation which has set people off in new directions, in some cases more creative and fulfilling than their previous frenetic farrago of haste and upheaval. They have found satisfaction in doing some of the things they never used to have time for, or rather make time for; listening to more music, enjoying the richness of nature, or writing poetry. Others have enjoyed the satisfaction of becoming masters of their own destiny, by starting their own small businesses in which they can make the decisions and see them through to fruition rather than labouring under the creatively stifling atmosphere of work in a large impersonal industry.

Warning Signs

There are, of course, a large number of people who positively thrive on pressure and enjoy the cut and thrust of competition. They are stimulated by moving in the fast lane of life. It keeps their minds sharp and their creative drive in a high gear. There is no doubt that the progress of industry and at least some artistic endeavour has been the product of these qualities. This is fine for the person who is sufficiently well-tuned to maintain the pace but when the warning lights start flashing it may be time to slow down and take stock of the situation.

The danger signs for impending angina, or heart-disease, are easy to overlook when one is being swept along by events and misguided enthusiasm. The most common early warning is weariness. The feeling of being overburdened by a variety of circumstances including conflicts at home or in work, overwhelming responsibility, or disturbance of routine.

For a person working effectively at high pitch, but without much reserve, a change in the daily pattern of events, a period of greater responsibility or illness and feuds in the family, may pull them into decline — the start of the downward slope on the Function Curve.

When things start to slip the inevitable course of action is to try harder to keep up. Longer hours than necessary are worked with less effect but the added effort only aggravates the fatigue and the person gets swept into the vortex of the vicious circle described earlier, in which they lose their self-awareness, self-control, and possibly self-respect. That is when they become more vulnerable to environmental factors such as climatic changes and economic pressures.

A Way Out

It is very easy to feel trapped in this web of misfortune, believing oneself to be the victim of circumstance, but recognition of the warning signs should not be too difficult and most people have the capacity to extricate themselves from their position of vulnerability.

A recognition of the destructive nature of one's lifestyle is a major step to progress and, provided one can understand the process and be sufficiently well-informed about the ways of coping more effectively, there need be none of the anxiety that goes with ignorance and uncertainty.

Angina very often starts when life has got out of control in all sorts of ways but it is surprising how much one can take it in hand and bring it back in the direction you wish to go. You may have to choose a different route but the important thing is that your hands should be on the steering wheel.

3.

Learning to Cope

Angina often comes as a surprise to the people it afflicts. They go careering through life taking their health for granted and are amazed when the chest pain strikes them down. Everyone has heard of a heart attack victim who 'never had a day's illness in his life'. Some people start getting anginal pains without any warnings. The physical decline of the heart and coronary arteries may advance for years without obvious symptoms but, quite often, it is a case of not recognizing the danger signals.

Tiredness is taken for granted; a frenetic way of doing things is fashionable, and the aggressive drive of the successful draws admiration. These qualities are well tolerated by the physically fit, structurally sound, and nutritionally well-balanced body, but not everyone is blessed with such attributes.

It is worth conducting an audit of your lifestyle to see whether you are really locked into a self-destructive patten. Ask yourself the following questions, ticking under yes or no accordingly:-

LIFE-STYLE AUDIT

| | YES | NO |

- Do you waken in the morning feeling tired?

- Do you suffer from insomnia?

- Do you have working lunches and business dinners?

- Is your working life frequented by appointments and deadlines?

- Do you cancel social engagements or rearrange holidays to accommodate business functions?

- Do you regularly stay late at the office or take work home?

- Do you commute at peak travel times?

- Do you have frequent disagreements in the home with spouse, children, or in-laws?

- Have you been through recent life change events

such as bereavement,
divorce, serious illness in
the family, house moves,
or change of work?

• Do you play to win?

Admittedly these are pretty loaded questions taken at random but they might provoke a little thought about the way you conduct your life. If you scored three or more yes's you are probably on the way to some type of breakdown in your health unless you are endowed with a good genetic background, mental resilience and healthy eating habits. Changes can be introduced on all fronts given the will, so it is worth thinking about some of the following suggestions. If you can act on them you may well find that you get more out of life in the long run, apart from ensuring simply that you get more life.

If it seems impossible to change a particular facet of your life, perhaps in terms of work routine, or home pressures, then don't allow that to be a source of anxiety. There may be many other ways in which you can reduce the risks.

Food

There are many degrees of change for the better which you can make with your diet. Some people still argue that food has little influence on angina, and certainly there is a great deal of confusion about what is good or bad. Nevertheless, there is mounting evidence for the role of some commonly consumed foods in causing heart-disease and angina. Furthermore, poor quality nutrition impairs the energy of the brain and nervous system which undermines our ability to cope with life's other brickbats.

The most important thing about food is the fact that we do have some control over it. We can do little about our genetic endowment, and may find it difficult to extricate ourselves from the web of wearying work and relentless personal pressures, but we can at least decide what food and drink we put in our mouths.

In Chapter 5 we shall take a closer look at ways in which simple changes can be introduced to your diet. Meanwhile the conditions under which you eat your food, particularly in relation to work, may bear closer scrutiny.

Keeping Work in its Place

The pressures of the workplace are frequently a cause of anxiety and tension in an environment which should be one of imaginative fulfilment. Most jobs have their hectic or worrying moments and if they don't they are likely to be monotonous and boring which is probably worse. At least challenges sharpen the mind and stimulate the creative capacity, provided one can resolve them satisfactorily. It is when the pressures of time and failure start to gain the upper hand that trouble begins.

The most common work-related threats to heart health arise from having too much for one's capabilities or for the time available. The sense of guilt in failing to keep abreast induces more fatiguing effort as well as anxiety about one's ability to hold the job down. This may be a particular concern for those in large organizations where competition for places of executive responsibility is great.

The first step to reform is to set more realistic targets both collectively and individually. Most people aim to do more than they achieve, whether at work, or in the home, but many accept that what doesn't get done simply has to wait until another day. The great art of leading a busy life is to be able to put off until tomorrow what should be done today — without feeling guilty about it.

Accessible Targets

It may help to plan out the day or week in advance. Write down the day's tasks, highlighting those which are of greatest urgency. You may even find it useful to allocate the times for these. Invariably some will run over the allocation and push others back on the timetable. The jobs which don't get done may have to be carried forward to subsequent days. Some may be put off for weeks in this way but if they are not too urgent you know they will get done eventually.

When the priority jobs have been done it is sometimes worth devoting a certain amount of time to most of the others on the list, even if they cannot be completed. In this way progress is being made on all fronts, which can be reassuring. Equally the sense of achievement in marking off completed tasks is conducive to greater peace of mind. Remember to leave time in each day for creative thinking.

Most successful people who keep control of their work plan their days in some way rather than approaching things haphazardly as they come along, but the important thing about planning is that you remain in control, and there is then much less likelihood of arousing tensions which might precipitate an angina attack. The well-organized person can achieve a great deal, but don't forget to be realistic about what you take on. There is a limit to the amount of balls which even the most skilful juggler can keep in the air at one time.

Spreading the Load

When responsibilities exceed capabilities it is important to be able to delegate. For Type A personalities, who like to retain control of all the switches, that may be difficult but it makes sense to free yourself of routine tasks in order to concentrate on things you do most effectively.

Planning your work day also means planning for leisure time. It is all too easy to allow a busy schedule to crowd out the periods of rest and recreation. Try to establish a regular time for exercise and other pastimes and, if at all possible, allow for a siesta. Making effective use of these spaces in your day will be the subject of the next chapter.

Working Meals

The working lunch seems to have become a necessary evil of competitive business. Business dinners are an established format, and now the hijacking of personal life by the demands of work has extended to the latest fashion for business breakfasts. There is no doubt that the informality and conviviality of food and drink provides a good background to discussion of important issues and, in a busy day, it is certainly a convenient way of utilizing time more effectively. But it isn't conducive to good digestion and what is bad for the digestion is ultimately bad for the heart.

If working meals are a regular feature of your business life it may be wise to restrict the number of engagements you have to fulfil in the course of a week. Unhurried breakfasts and leisurely lunches are an important ingredient of the angina sufferer's daily routine.

Commuting

One of the major hazards for the person with angina is the perpetual pressure of time. There simply isn't enough of it to do all the things they want to and, as they become overwhelmed by the inability to fit everything in, anginal attacks are more likely to occur.

Getting to work or reaching appointments on time is a major cause of arousal for some people, particularly when daily travel is punctuated by cancellations, delays, overcrowding, and traffic jams. The first essential is to plan sufficient time for your journey just as you plan other aspects of your day. Estimate the time it will take and allow at least 25% extra in case of unexpected delays. You can always occupy the spare time at the other end in some useful or pleasurable way.

Decide which form of transport is going to

give you the most peace of mind. If you drive you may have to face traffic jams, bad weather, and parking problems. Facing these with equanimity demands great reserves of patience and perseverence. On the other hand there are many people for whom their car is a haven — as one man put it, 'The moment I step into my car I am at home'. With the radio or some favourite tapes, a reliable, comfortable vehicle, and adequate time for your journey, you are insulated from most of the stresses of life for an hour or two (unless, of course, you have the doubtful luxury of a car phone!) with an opportunity for creative thought.

Commuting by train has the advantage of providing the opportunity to read, write, or for those precious catnaps, provided you don't have to spend too much time standing on station platforms or pushing yourself into the tube trains. Don't get yourself into the predicament of having to run for a train or bus — it is better to take your exercise without the anxiety which that entails!

Whatever way you travel to or from work, whether by car, bus, train, or plane, the golden rule, then, is to allow sufficient time for your journey so that you can look forward to it as a pleasant interlude in the day — an agreeble transition between workplace and home.

Avoiding Hassle in the Home

In some cases the home environment can become more highly charged than that of the work place. For the person recovering from a heart attack or learning to cope with angina the active participation of all members of the family is essential. Sharing domestic responsibilities can relieve the burden on the main home manager. Every task taken on in the house or garden by another member of the family is one less burden for the angina sufferer to face.

The trouble with angina is that you can appear to be quite well outwardly while all the tensions and spasms are building up inside, so people around you very soon start taking things for granted. If you do not want to become too hypochondriacal you may not wish to impose upon other members of the family. This can be particularly true of women sufferers. People assume that they are less likely to be victims but, whereas men are more likely to get a heart attack, angina is often the first sign of heart trouble in women.

Occupational Therapy

In some coronary care units, notably that at Charing Cross Hospital, London, the Occupational Therapist plays an important role in training heart attack and angina cases to lead more effective lives. Occupational Therapists have the skills to become aware of the behaviour patterns which lead to excessive arousal and exhaustion in their patients, teach them methods of relaxation and correct breathing, and encourage them to adopt more realistic goals. Patients are also encouraged to develop other interests and hobbies that will not impose excessive mental or physical demands — avoiding the element of competition.

There are many creative skills which can be taken up in the home, calling for some manual and mental dexterity without any of the tension-provoking aspects of the more competitive pastimes. In the early stages of recovery from angina, craftwork and diversionary mental pursuits are essential preparation for the more active programmes which will later build up the physical fitness of the heart and lungs. Above all they serve as a valuable diversion of the aggressive trends.

A Change of Attitude

Undoubtedly, the most important step towards recovery you can make will be a change of attitude. If you can dump your feelings of fear, anxiety and defeat and replace them with confidence in your own capacity for effective function, recognition of your potential for better health, and awareness of your body's physical needs, you will create the positive biochemical changes which encourage its anabolic rebuilding activities. Quite simply, positive thinking reduces negative functioning in our bodies.

In cultivating what has been described as 'the art of the possible' you will develop a mental outlook which is protective against the more damaging emotions. You will find it possible to proceed with quiet determination, secure in the knowledge that any setback you may experience is not a defeat but is laying the foundation of experience on which to build future success. You are, in a sense, oiling your feathers against failure, frustration and fatigue.

Getting Back to Normal

The first thing most people want after a heart attack or the onset of angina is to get back to 'normal'. If that, for you, means punishing schedules and inadequate rest, forget it! Remember that anginal symptoms, like many others, are well down the path of declining health. It will require time and careful management to rebuild your health and retrain your body.

This process must start with an appreciation of the role played by destructive patterns in your life, coming to terms with the changes in your health and using them as a basis for more constructive developments in personal care for the future. You will need to get adequate rest before introducing gentle physical training. The right point at which to start on a new phase in the programme of rehabilitation will vary from person to person and you will be guided in this by your doctor who can base his judgement on medical assessments such as blood-pressure and biochemistry.

So, surrender to the period of inactivity and resist the desire to do just a little bit here and the odd job there, before your medical adviser permits you to do so. Instead you can use the time to consider how you may plan your normal routine of work, food and recreation. When you do return to work it is preferable to start with only three days per week leaving the remaining two days for training schedules and rest.

A Space and Pace Programme

We can summarize the elements of your new lifestyle for coping with angina by creating a programme in which you make more space to work and play at your own (more realistic) pace.

- Plan your working day to realistic targets achieved at a realistic pace.
- Create space for rest and recreation.
- Ensure that you have adequate sleep and introduce a siesta.
- Don't allow deadlines to dominate your day; put off until tomorrow what should be done today.
- Avoid the feeling that you must 'keep up with the boys' — especially if you are a girl!

4.

Rest and Exercise

The economy of the heart and circulation depends, like any other, on the simple law of supply and demand. While the supply of blood reaching the heart muscle can meet its demands, it functions smoothly. If the demands outstrip the available oxygenated blood the heart weakens. On the other hand if the heart demands less and less, through the inertia of its owner, the coronary arteries will become accustomed to delivering less and less blood so it is ill-prepared for any unexpected activity.

The fitness of the heart is thus crucial for coping with the requirements of the body, whether physical or mental. Fitness is only achieved by regular exercise. The person who has developed angina has probably become rather unfit but it is possible to retrain the heart by well graduated activity.

To exercise effectively, though, you need adequate reserves of energy and, since the onset of angina usually marks the breaking point in a period of exhaustion, the first steps to recovery must be directed to ensuring that you get adequate rest.

THE THREE R S

So, your first requirement if you have angina is to develop proficiency in the three Rs — rest, relaxation and recreation. There is a difference between them. Rest means physical and mental inactivity and, usually, sleep. Relaxation is the art of letting go — of releasing muscular tensions and switching off the buzzing brain. Recreation may be more active for both mind and body and is, by definition, a pleasurable pastime; something which gives a diversion to the toil and turmoil of normal living.

It is surprising how many people go through life without being capable of getting the best value from these essentials. Because there are real physiological benefits to be derived from them, rest, relaxation and recreation are probably more important than the reading, writing and arithmetic which are regarded as such fundamentals of our education.

Benefits of Sleep

If you are a new recruit to the ranks of angina sufferers you will need to get plenty of rest. Indeed, for some time it may not have been a major feature of your life, but now it is essential. Rest gives the body the opportunity for recovery and building of reserves. You will probably be aware of great tiredness. This is very noticeable after heart attacks and a frequent accompaniment of angina. The body is expressing its profound need for sleep.

During sleep the balance of the body's functions shifts to anabolism — the building of

reserves by cell division and protein synthesis.
Sleep positively inhibits the production of
cortisol and the catecholamines, the hormones
of activity and arousal. On the other hand there
are higher levels of the human growth hormone
(HGH) which encourages the build-up of protein
reserves and mobilizes the fatty acids in the
body to provide more energy. HGH also lowers
cholesterol levels.

It is also known that damaged tissues heal
more quickly during sleep, whatever the type of
injury. So both the coronary artery walls and the
oxygen-deprived heart muscles will derive
benefits from adequate sleep.

During a normal night's slumber we pass
through different levels of consciousness. These
have been monitored in numerous experiments
in which volunteers have slept with electrodes
taped all over their heads to measure the
electrical activity of the brain. These
electroencephalographic (EEG) readings show
that there are cycles of brain activity, each of
which appears to play an important role in our
processes of regeneration and readjustment. As
we fall asleep the amplitude of brain waves
slowly becomes greater and we experience
vague images and occasional muscle twitches.
Within twenty or thirty minutes we sink into a
stage of large slow brain waves eventually
reaching a deep sleep in which hormonal activity
is greatest, with higher levels of, for example,
the growth hormone.

The deep Stage IV sleep occurs mostly in the
early part of the night, particularly before
midnight, so, for the young at least, the old

maxim about the hours of sleep before midnight being the most beneficial has some scientific basis. Subjects who have been deprived of Stage IV sleep, under experimental conditions, developed malaise, apathy, and depression.

In the early hours of the morning we pass back through Stages III and II, with longer spells of increased brain activity, particularly in the form of dreams. This is described as REM sleep, because of the rapid eye movements which occur at this time. During REM sleep the body starts to release small spurts of cortisol and adrenalin so it is being prepared for more activity. It is in this phase that angina sufferers will sometimes awaken suddenly with pain and shortness of breath.

This does not mean that REM sleep is bad; in fact it serves the valuable function of allowing our brains to sift and file the images and experiences of the recent past. People deprived of REM sleep become irritable and anxious, a process likely to be compounded, in the long term, by the use of excessive alcohol and drugs, which tend to suppress this phase of our slumbers.

This poses something of a dilemma for the person who has difficulty in sleeping, for they miss out on the important body synchronizing and harmonizing function which sleep provides if they have to rely on sleeping tablets and other powerful tranquillizers.

Aids to Better Sleep
The complex rhythms of our bodies, with the fluctuations of our physiology, continue, of

course, throughout the day and night. This is why we are so susceptible to changes of time-zone when we travel, or to the twenty-four hour cycles when we work on night shifts or irregular hours. For some people the disturbance of brain cycles becomes an almost permanent feature resulting in the inability to fall asleep at a reasonable hour, or to stay asleep for long enough to feel rested.

If you are unfortunate enough to be an insomniac there are several ways in which you may be able to improve your sleep pattern without resorting to the drugs which are so habit-forming and disorientating in their side-effects. One of the simplest procedures you can carry out at home is hydrotherapy. In German spas, where people are given various types of water treatments, the patients are encouraged to paddle through tanks of cold water before retiring for the night. Spraying or sponging the lower legs with cold water for two or three minutes before drying with a rough towel helps to balance the circulation, drawing the blood away from the upper part of the body and head. You can also try this if you wake in the night.

Gentle exercise, such as a short walk in the fresh air, is also helpful if the brain has become overactive with working, watching TV, or other matters requiring concentration in the evening.

Warm drinks also draw the blood down provided they are non-stimulating and nourishing. Herb teas, such as chamomile and peppermint, are pleasant and settling. It is very important to avoid stimulants, such as coffee or strong tea, which have higher levels of caffeine.

Nutrition and Sleep

The restless rhythms of the brain may sometimes be the result of biochemical insufficiencies arising through poor nutrition. More detailed consideration of food requirements will be given in the next chapter. There are some supplements which appear to help those with insomnia.

Magnesium is involved in energy metabolism and is necessary for proper functioning of nerves and muscles including those of the heart. Magnesium is found in fresh green vegetables, raw wheat-germ, soya beans, apples, nuts and seeds. Supplement your intake with Dolomite tablets, a natural combination of magnesium and calcium with trace elements.

Calcium has special actions in nervous tissue. It is necessary for correct transmission of impulses and deficiencies may result in nervous irritability, twitchiness and muscle cramps. Calcium is present in nuts, seeds, dairy foods, soya milk and seafood. Use Dolomite as a supplement or a natural preparation of calcium phosphate.

Potassium regulates the mineral balance of the heart muscles and plays an important role in nervous system function. It is found in all vegetables, wholegrains, sunflower seeds, potatoes, grapes and bananas. Supplement potassium with a biologically balanced compound preparation.

Vitamin B complex is a major nutrient in the functional physiology of the nervous system, as well as playing an important role in energy production. The B vitamins are present in Brewer's yeast and wholegrain cereals such as brown rice and whole wheat. Brewer's yeast may be used as a supplement but a yeast free B complex supplement is also available for people who do not cope well with yeast preparations.

Tryptophan is an essential amino acid which has been found to be of value in the treatment of insomnia. The amino acids are the basic constituents of protein. Foods richest in tryptophan are soya, cottage cheese, fish, liver, pumpkin and sesame seeds. Supplements of tryptophan should only be taken with the guidance of your doctor or a naturopath, since there are important considerations of dosage and interactions with other nutrients.

Herbal preparations using combinations of Skullcap, Valerian and Passion Flower are nourishing and calming to the nervous system and may be used to aid sleep. Extract of Cactus is sometimes added to support the functions of the heart. (See Chapters 5 and 6.)

Restoring Siesta Time

In a day of perpetual pressure from the responsibilities of work, or the routine of the domestic round, a short pause is a precious opportunity to switch into a gentler rhythm and reduce the level of tension in the body. An ideal way to do this is to introduce a siesta. In the industrialized countries, with cooler climates, we have become so preoccupied with the 'work ethic' that it is almost considered a sin to take a lunch break, let alone make it long enough to have a rest. There doesn't have to be tropical heat to justify a noonday nap.

All you need are ten or fifteen minutes in which to sit quietly, or better still, to stretch out in a comfortable position. If you go through a simple relaxation routine such as that described on page 67 you will reduce the physical and mental tensions, and provide a few minutes welcome rest and regeneration for your body. You may doze off, if only for five minutes or so, but it will take the brain into Stage II sleep, the REM stage, which is at least restful. Even catnaps, taken at other times of the day, on the train, or in a plane, take you into Stage II, so they can be valuable.

Relaxation
Some people are reluctant to rest in the daytime because they have enough trouble getting to sleep at night. If you are among these you may benefit by practising some form of relaxation. Even if you are fortunate enough to sleep well, the ability to let go physically and mentally is a skill in which every angina patient needs instruction. It is surprising how many of us harbour tensions of which we are not aware.

Relaxation reduces the level of arousal and brings down the blood-pressure. The positive benefits of relaxation were demonstrated in a study carried out by Dr Chandra Patel, and reported in the *British Medical Journal* (Volume

290). She studied 1,268 men and women employed in one industry, so their work environment was basically similar. When they were screened for blood-pressure and cholesterol levels, 192 were found to have the risk factors for heart-disease — moderately raised blood-pressure and cholesterol levels, and the smoking habit.

These risk factor patients were divided into two groups, one of which was a control group and the other a treatment group. All the patients were given an educational leaflet which described the importance of reducing smoking and fat intake and lowering the blood-pressure. The treatment group, however, were also given one hour per week of instruction in breathing, relaxation, meditation, and stress reduction.

When monitored at eight weeks and eight months after commencement of the programme a significant reduction of blood-pressure was noted in the treatment group. This difference was maintained when the groups were followed up four years later and by then more of the controls had had angina and treatment for blood-pressure than the relaxation group.

There are many different ways of releasing physical and mental tensions, ranging from meditation to the methods linked to exercise systems such as yoga and T'ai chi. The best systems encourage you to develop an awareness of your tensions and promote the release of these by gentle breathing.

Biofeedback methods, for example, employ simple electrical instruments which register the changes in the skin resistance as you reduce muscle tensions. An audible signal or a reading on the gauge tells you when you are letting go sufficiently. In autogenic training a series of exercises in which the subject concentrates on verbal instructions lead to a state of greater physical relaxation. These techniques require instruction and expert guidance and it is a good idea to join a class or get individual tuition if this is available near you.

A particularly easy system to practise at home is the method developed by L.E. Eeman, which is taught by many naturopaths. This method uses breathing to induce relaxation but you adopt a position in which the natural polarity of the body is considered. The energies are encouraged to flow freely instead of being obstructed, as they so often are, by muscular tensions and 'holding on'. You can go through the routine, which is described opposite, almost anywhere if you have about ten minutes to spare. Although it is best performed lying flat you may still follow the pattern of breathing and letting go in an armchair.

Try and practise your relaxation routine every day. At first there may be areas of your body, especially the neck and shoulders, which do not want to let go. Keep sending the ideas to them though and, after a few twitches and quivers, they may release. It is helpful to work through the Eeman Technique before you go to sleep at night. When you have been right through the body turn to your normal sleeping position, if you haven't already dropped off!

A RELAXATION ROUTINE

Object
Complete relaxation of voluntary muscles to enable reduction of waste products produced by their activity, and to reduce oxygen demands. Physical relaxation promotes mental calm.

Time required
Five to ten minutes minimum, or as a preliminary to night sleep.

Place
Anywhere you can lie flat comfortably, e.g., bed, or a rug on the floor.

How to relax
(Until you are familiar with the routine, try and get a friend to read this through as you follow it.)

Remove shoes and loosen tight clothing. Lie on your back on a comfortable surface. A small cushion or pillow may support the neck and head.

Lay your hands across the abdomen, with the fingers lightly interlaced, and arms resting on the bed.

Breathe in deeply, filling the abdomen first (diaphragmatic breathing), and then sigh out and repeat this a few times, audibly if it helps.

Now allow the breathing to continue at its own pace and depth but, as you sigh out, concentrate on one part of your body, letting go with each breath. Start with the ankles and feet, letting them flop outwards where gravity takes them. Feel the joints loosening.

Move onto the legs for the next breath or two, and work up your body, conveying the idea of letting go, as you come to each part, even if it won't quite relax as well as you would like it to.

Once you feel that the ankles, legs, and knees are relaxed, forget them and move up in this order:.

hips and thighs — think particularly of the inner thigh muscles, which are often tense as a subconscious protector of the genital organs;

hands and forearms — feel the small muscles and joints in the fingers relaxing;

abdomen — let it sag;

chest — feel the muscles between the ribs letting go:

the whole back, from the buttocks up to the shoulders — feel them sinking and spreading on to the bed;

neck and shoulders — often difficult to let go but send the message through and it will eventually get there;

head and face — feel the eyes sinking back into their sockets, jaw muscles slacken, mouth may fall open.

With one or two deeper breaths and sighs feel the whole body sinking into deeper relaxation — sigh.........sink.........and sag.

Your friend can test your relaxation by rolling the legs, or lifting up an arm and letting it drop. You won't hurt yourself if you are quite relaxed.

When you are really floppy just lie and think of green countryside and a blue sky — the colours which aid relaxation. Let your breathing proceed at its own pace; it will sometimes slow right down, or occasionally a deeper sigh will want to come through. Allow any little muscular twitches and jerks to take their course. They are just due to tension being released. Rest for a while like this and you may even fall asleep.

Before you rise

Remember the cat; it never leaps up unless it is disturbed. It stretches, a little at a time, to gradually increase the circulation to the muscles ready for more action. You should try and do the same.

Stretch your arms and legs, and breathe a little more deeply, to get the muscles into action, and circulate the oxygen.

You will now feel more rested with an improved circulation and better energy.

EXERCISE

One of the anxieties of the anginal person is that exercise will induce an attack. They become apprehensive about exertion and, as a consequence, seldom give the heart and the other muscles sufficient activity to remain well conditioned. On balance exercise is beneficial if it is conducted without undue duress.

A well-designed programme of exercise serves

not only to increase your physical capacity but also to discharge aggressive energy and the tension which this generates. When the mind has been whirring and you have been faced by the frustrations which are part of any working day the muscles are automatically prepared to fight or run away. As you probably don't do either they become tense, unless there is some physical outlet like the Japanese workers' punchbag. But even if your boss is unbearable don't start thumping his effigy just yet! Until your heart is better trained it may not appreciate the sudden call to arms.

Reconditioning the Heart

The benefits of exercise to the heart are indirect. It is the oxygen-demanding skeletal muscles which do the work, moving the arms, legs and chest. As the demand increases, so does the difference between oxygen in the arteries on its way to the muscles, and in the veins, coming back. As the heart becomes more efficient at meeting these demands the amount of exercise you can perform before provoking an angina attack increases.

Regular exercise also promotes weight loss, lowers the blood-pressure and reduces the levels of cholesterol and triglycerides, all of which is good news for angina subjects. The HDL cholesterol, which helps to keep the fats moving, is increased by exercise.

Exercise does tend to raise the adrenalin levels but since there is proper discharge in muscular activity the general effect is to increase alertness rather than create excessive tension.

There are, therefore, enormous psychological benefits to be derived from regular physical activity.

Fitness and Well-Being

There are various types of fitness and there is rarely an athlete who can claim proficiency in all. Flexibility, muscle strength, muscle endurance, speed, balance, agility and co-ordination all call for the development of different neuromuscular skills according to the particular athletic pursuit. The acrobat, weightlifter, dancer and marathon runner place different demands upon their bodies, and there are probably few angina sufferers who would aspire to their highly-conditioned state.

The main objective is not so much peak level fitness but all round well-being which can be achieved by a more varied programme of exercise. That needs to incorporate physical activity which is aerobic — not the crazed jerking around to strident screams competing with deafening muzak which has been the vogue in recent years — but exercise which develops heart and lung fitness in a gradual way, geared to individual capabilities. It involves dynamic activity, such as walking, jogging and swimming, in which the muscles work while using oxygen to convert food to energy.

The type of exercise which keeps the muscles moving and the lungs expanding and contracting is called *isotonic*. For angina patients it is infinitely preferable to *isometric* exercise in which the muscles are static a lot of the time, with the breathing restricted or held.

This happens in, for example, weight lifting, pulling and pushing, or carrying without much movement, which makes heavy demands on the heart and increases the blood-pressure. Those exercises which make sudden demands upon the left ventricle, by bursts of activity, as in squash, also need to be avoided.

Training

The art of good exercise is to promote the reserve of the left ventricle of the heart. Your doctor will be able to gauge more or less when your heart has the flexibility to cope with a graduated training programme. This may not be until after some weeks of rest, learning to 'let go' sufficiently not to induce angina.

Dr Peter Nixon, of Charing Cross Hospital, London, gives the following prescription to patients who have had heart attacks and they must fulfil it before they are able to start training:

> Not once tired, not once angry, not once uncomfortable under time pressure and not one attack of angina during the next two months.

He also recommends that no vigorous physical training should be undertaken until patients are able to cope without beta-blocking drugs, or glyceryl trinitrate. The heart is slowed or relaxed by these drugs and tends to meet the demands of exercise by dilating instead of accelerating naturally. The dilatation may ultimately weaken the heart. The blood-pressure of people on such medicines tends to fall after exercise.

You may have access to a gymnasium or fitness centre where they have a circuit training routine suitable for people with heart problems, but make sure there is some supervision and avoid any competitive element, such as attempts to improve speed or increase resistance too rapidly in the equipment you use. Equipment is not essential for training, however, as there are many forms of exercise which increase the stamina of heart and lungs.

All you really need is a good pair of legs because one of the most effective exercises is walking. It would probably be best to start with short walks and increase the distance gradually. If they go well you can consider introducing some gentle jogging. You could start by jogging fifteen or twenty yards periodically while out walking and build up from there.

Other possibilities are swimming and cycling, but whatever you prefer to do it must be an activity which sustains regular motion with freedom of the breathing mechanisms.

How Much Exercise?

If you decide on a particular exercise routine, or simply walking, it is important to spread the activity through the week. Infrequent but prolonged bursts of exercise achieve little more than exhaustion of the heart. More frequent short rounds of activity, say twenty minutes three times a week, are much more effective in developing stamina and vital capacity.

You can monitor the amount of exercise of which you are capable by your pulse rate. It is useful to get into the habit of checking your pulse before and after exercising. The pulse is most easily felt over the radial artery at the wrist. Place the fingertips of your left hand in the depression just below the mound of your thumb on the inner side of the right wrist. You can usually feel the beat which you should count for one minute.

Effective exercise needs to raise the pulse rate to 60 or 70% of its possible maximum. As a general rule the maximum healthy heart beat attainable is equivalent to 220 beats per minute minus your age in years. A 50 year old man would, therefore, be able to aim for:

$$220 - 50 = 170 \times 60\% = 102 \text{ beats/minute}$$

When you start your exercise programme you should not let the pulse exceed the 60 – 65% of maximum speed, but as you become fitter the heart is able to meet greater demands by faster beats, up to 85% of the maximum. The 50 year-old starting his exercise programme by taking the pulse rate to around 102 beats per minute, will, after some weeks, probably be able to take it to 145 per minute without inducing an angina attack. But there will be big variations in exercise tolerance from person to person depending on a variety of other things, such as stress, weight and nutritional state. There may also be other physical restraints such as arthritis and back ache. These can generally be considerably relieved without resorting to drugs, so do consult an osteopath, chiropractor or acupuncturist for help.

Increasing Capacity

The key to effective heart/lung exercise is to increase the capacity rather than trying to step up the pace. Aim to walk, run or swim a greater distance as you become fitter, but let time be the secondary factor. If you are working to a timed schedule, say 20 minutes every two days, you will inevitably get faster as you achieve more but don't attempt to race against yourself or anyone else.

Another precaution is to recognize your limitations when you become fitter. There is often a point at which your perception of well-being outstrips your real physical capabilities. There Is then the risk of doing too much too soon. After a week or two of regular exercise there is a feeling of euphoria induced by the greater output of adrenalin. One may then be tempted to undertake bursts of physical exertion which might precipitate angina in a heart not yet fit enough to meet the body's demands.

Other Forms of Exercise

So far we have thought about active aerobic forms of exercise which have a definite training effect. Brisk walking, jogging or swimming develop physical fitness and stamina but there are gentler forms of exercise which increase flexibility, encourage better breathing and improve the circulation, promoting oxygenation of all body cells. These are the systems which originated mainly in the Orient — yoga, from the Indian subcontinent, and T'ai chi and Qi gong, from China.

Their respiratory benefits — particularly valuable for people who hyperventilate — derive from the emphasis on co-ordinating breathing with the movements. The exercises consist of a series of moving postures, called *asanas* in the yoga system, which are performed quite slowly.

There are many different forms of yoga, T'ai chi and Qi gong and it is wise to attend a class with an experienced teacher. Most towns and cities have yoga classes, often run in conjunction with adult education institutions, and T'ai chi and Qi gong are increasingly available. It is, however, possible to learn a few simple routines from a good instruction book.

The sequence described here is based on several simple yoga postures and forms a routine known as Salutation to the Sun. It combines breathing with movements which exercise all parts of the body to promote better oxygenation of the heart, lungs and other organs, increase the circulation and drainage of the abdominal organs, stretch the spinal column, loosen the other joints and muscles and tonify the nervous system. The Salutation to the Sun is a good sequence to perform first thing in the morning as it only takes a few minutes and helps to get the body energy moving.

Breathing Well
Before commencing this, or any other system of exercise, poise yourself with a little gentle breathing. When breathing with yoga or T'ai chi postures you should try to let the air in and out rather than forcing it through the nostrils in a

sniffing fashion. Open the back of the nose as you breathe in and you will become aware of air reaching the sinuses. Imagine the cavities of the sinuses opening to receive life-giving oxygen. Inhale it right to the base of the lungs, expanding the lower ribs and diaphragm before filling the upper lungs. Then exhale a little more forcefully, depressing the rib cage until you have got all the air out. You need to do this before breathing in again. The lower lungs fill first and empty last in this method, known as abdominal breathing.

It may help to place your hands at the sides of the lower ribs with fingers pointing together over the upper abdomen so that you can feel the expansion and contraction. As you breathe in the fingers will move apart. And then they move together again as you breathe out and the ribs compress. Practising abdominal breathing prevents the tense upper chest breathing, often seen in asthmatics, which puts more strain on the heart. When you have established a good breathing rhythm you can start this simple yoga routine. You do need to be reasonably supple to perform this routine so, if you are overweight or if your blood-pressure is high, it would be better to check with your practitioner before attempting it.

SALUTATION TO THE SUN

Wear loose or comfortable clothing. Shorts, tracksuits, pyjamas or, if warm enough, nakedness, are equally suitable.

1. Stand with bare feet firmly on the floor about 9 inches apart, knees very slightly bent, body upright but comfortably poised with neck and shoulders relaxed. Face the east, if possible, and exercise before an open window if you are indoors.

2. Place the palms of the hands together in front of the chest with your elbows forward so that the wrists are at right angles. Breathe out slowly.

3. As you breathe in again (remember to open the sinuses) link your thumbs and turn the palms of the hands to the front. Stretch the arms and the hands forwards and up over your head, then lean back as far as you can comfortably go.

4. Now bend forwards with arms outstretched and reach towards your toes, breathing out as you do so. You don't need to keep the legs straight, nor is it necessary to reach the floor if you are not supple enough. Just bend over as far as you can with the head tucked under towards your knees.

5. Next stretch your right foot and leg out behind you along the floor while you bend the left knee and place your hands on the floor in front of you. Stretch your arms and bend the head back as you breathe in. This should become one smooth movement.

6. Bring the left foot back level with the right, bend the head forward and push your bottom up into the air. You are now in an

inverted 'V'. This movement is done fairly quickly while you hold your breath.

7. Breathe out as you bend your arms and lower your body until your toes, knees, chest and forehead are touching the floor.

8. Breathe in again as you stretch the arms, pushing your head and shoulders back, but with the legs and feet still contacting the floor.

9. Draw the feet up so that you are in the inverted 'V' position again, breathing out as you do it.

10. Now bring the right foot up beneath your chest keeping the left stretched out behind you, bending back neck and shoulders as you breathe in.

11. Draw the left foot up beside the right to bring you into the bent double position again. Breathe out while you do this.

12. Breathe in again as you straighten up and bend back with arms over the head.

13. Return to the starting position with the hands in the prayer attitude again. You can repeat the sequence or relax the arms to the standing position.

5.

Food and Drink

The whole issue of food for healthy hearts hinges on its wholeness. What we eat should be, as far as possible, near its whole natural state to provide us with the nutritional elements essential for healthy function.

If they are available in adequate quantity the excesses of this or that type of food assume secondary importance since the body will be better able to cope with them and will, in any case, be less likely to have more than is good for its health. The food which furnishes our bodies most efficiently with vitamins, minerals and trace elements will tend to be higher in fibre and lower in fats and sugars — the trouble makers — and with optimum nutrition (the correct balance of nutrients for our individual needs) we will be better equipped to digest the less suitable ingredients of the diet, so they will cause little harm.

The battle over food and heart-disease rages between those who say that what we eat has little to do with it, and those for whom it is the primary risk factor. The poor angina victim is caught in the cross-fire of confusion over cholesterol, fats in general, sugar, fibre, alcohol and salt. For many years the pattern was one of pronouncements by one set of experts and denials by another, some of whom later had the wisdom to look more closely at the question, carry out research, and change their opinions in the light of the evidence they produced.

Whilst they are by no means the only factor, there is now no doubt that eating habits play a significant part in the onset of heart-disease. In the USA there has been a definite reduction in the number of heart attacks since a campaign to reduce consumption of animal fats was introduced. In the UK, the Committee on Medical Aspects of Food Policy (COMA) finally woke up in 1984 to the importance of reducing fat, sugar and salt in our diets and recommended changes in our national eating habits accordingly.

In spite of this there are still 'experts' who maintain that animal fats and sugar are essential nutrients which are harmless. They are sometimes most convincing and persuasive in their arguments until one realizes that they have been sponsored by the dairy industry or the sugar manufacturers!

Optimum Nutrition

Long before we knew anything about the different types of cholesterol, or the hazards of refined sugars in the diet, the naturopaths, and a few nutritionally orientated doctors, were advocating a diet low in fats, sugar and salt, consisting instead of a predominance of fresh raw fruit and vegetables, with wholegrain produce, as the most suitable for the management and prevention of heart disorders.

Their aim was optimum nutrition, which means the most appropriate nutrients in appropriate amounts for each individual's needs. Our personal nutritional requirements can vary considerably, so one person may need rather more of a vitamin or mineral to maintain a biochemical function than another. Some people can cope with fats or sugars more efficiently than others. These variations may be determined by a number of things, ranging from constitution or body type (i.e., tall thin ones have different requirements from short fat ones) to genetic predispositions. There is, for example, an inherited disorder of fat metabolism, known as familial hypercholesterolaemia, which makes some people produce abnormal amounts of cholesterol. People with this condition do need to be extra careful to limit their intake of fatty and sugary foods and should also have supplements, such as vitamin E, to prevent coagulation of blood fats.

Why do some foods, often the ones we enjoy most, cause such problems? One reason is that we may tend to eat too much of those which are naturally difficult for our bodies to deal with, but the second, more important, reason is that they have often been processed or modified from the natural form in which we would be able to use them efficiently. A third important consideration is that through many years of unsuitable nutrition deficient in the elements which maintain our biochemical functions, we gradually lose the capacity to cope with these foods effectively anyway.

Figure 5: Molecular Structure of Fats

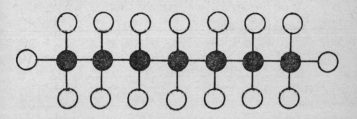

Saturated or
'hard' fats have each carbon atom
fully occupied by hydrogen atoms.

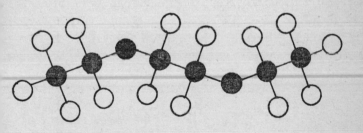

Polyunsaturated or
'soft' fats have several
free carbon atoms which makes
them more flexible.

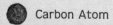 Carbon Atom   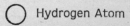 Hydrogen Atom

Fats

Fats have become more famous as a factor in heart-disease than as an essential food. All fats are composed of fatty acids, some of which are 'essential' ingredients of the daily diet because we cannot make them ourselves. These essential fatty acids are necessary to manufacture bile, nourish the nerves and carry vitamins, and are usually liquid at room temperature. They are described as the unsaturated fatty acids and stay in solution because of their molecular structure which leaves two or more of their carbon atoms unattached to a hydrogen atom, that is the molecule is not saturated with hydrogen atoms. Those with four or more vacancies for hydrogen atoms are called polyunsaturated fatty acids and are found in vegetable or seed oils, such as corn oil or sunflower seed oil.

The harder fats, such as butter, cheese and meats, are high in saturated fatty acids, so-called because all available carbon atoms are occupied by a hydrogen. They are, therefore, more difficult to break down in the body so their principle ingredient, cholesterol, tends to form a so-called buffy coat, like a greasy film, on the walls of the red blood cells, preventing them from carrying sufficient oxygen.

Dr G. Douglas Talbot, a cardiac consultant to the US space programmes, has expressed the view that one requires 34% more oxygen when the blood fat levels are raised. The reduced oxygen carrying capacity of the red cells may account for the sluggishness and drowsiness, or even chest pain, which some angina patients experience after a fatty meal. It may also cause a clumping and stickiness of the platelets which leads to deposits and obstructions in the arteries.

Dr R. Swank, at the University of Oregon Medical School, made a study of the blood after fatty meals. He noticed a clumping of the red blood cells (sometimes even the white cells, some of which maintain our immune system functions) but the adhesiveness cleared as the fatty particles were reduced. Just to show that dietary fats can be tolerated with varying degrees of efficiency, Drs Friedman and Rosenbaum, who classified the Type A and Type B personalities, found that the greatest clumping of blood cells occurred in those under the greatest time pressure.

Dietary Fat Trial

The fact that fat in the diet affects the incidence of heart-disease has been fairly conclusively demonstrated in trials carried out in various parts of the world. An interesting comparison was made between the diets of southern Italians, which consist primarily of pastas with olive oil (higher in unsaturated fatty acids) and people in north Finland, where saturated fat accounts for nearly half the total calorie intake.

For six weeks the Finnish families ate the Mediterranean diet and at the end of this period it was found that the level of their blood fats fell by an average of 22%. Their blood pressures also reduced whilst following the diets, only to increase again when they returned to more animal fats.

As part of the same trial southern Italian families spent six weeks on the typical diet of their northern countrymen, to determine whether racial differences might be significant. Northern Italians eat more refined carbohydrates and animal fats and on this diet the cholesterol levels of the southern Italians increased by 15%.

There are, of course, contradictory reports which should be noted. For example, in Switzerland the rate of heart attacks fell by 43% in women and 22% in men in the 25 years up to 1976, in spite of the fact that consumption of animal fats rose. (Could it be that patterns of exercise or levels of stress changed in some way during that time?) Scotland has the highest coronary heart-disease death rate in the world but a lower fat intake than in other parts of the UK.

Some of the contradictions may be accounted for by the differences in the types of cholesterol we ingest. The saturated fats contain a higher proportion of the type known as low density lipoprotein (LDL cholesterol) whilst the body needs to have a higher proportion of high density lipoprotein (HDL) found in the polyunsaturated fats. The ratio of the two types can, in fact, form a basis for predicting the risk of heart-disease. People with a cholesterol to HDL ratio of 5:1 have been found to be average risk, whilst a ratio of 3:1 (about 180mg cholesterol to 60mg HDL) reduces the risk of heart-disease by one half.

Reducing Your Fat Intake

Most people's dietary fat comes from foods which are high in saturated fatty acids, the LDL cholesterol. The following foods in the average diet can contain up to 90% saturated fat: milk and cream, cheese, butter, margarine, cooking fats, meat and meat products, baked goods with shortening, salad dressings, fried food.

You can see that hard fats crop up in a number of disguises. The vegetable oils from which many margarines are made, for example, are subjected to a process known as hydrogenation, in which hydrogen atoms are added to the molecular structure of the fat to make it solid at room temperature. These create another form of fat known as the trans-fatty acids. It is, therefore, necessary to treat most margarines in the same way as butter and, since they often have a high salt content as well, you may be better off with low-salt butter in moderation.

It is the polyunsaturates which help to keep all our fats moving, and are therefore less likely to clog the coronaries, so look for vegetable oil margarines which are labelled 'high in polyunsaturates'. (Some health food stores sell a German sunflower-oil margarine which is prepared without hydrogenation and is free of added salt).

In Table 1 you will see a number of ways in which you may replace the fattier ingredients of an average diet with agreeable alternatives.

Cholesterol levels are not only affected by our fat intake. Dietary cholesterol accounts for only 10% of total blood cholesterol; the other 90% is

Table 1

Fatty food	Substitute
Milk	Skimmed milk, soya milk, tofu.
Cream	Goat's milk yogurt, tofu, cashew nut or almond cream.
Butter	Polyunsaturated (unhydrogenated) margarine.
Cheeses, hard and high fat.	Curd or cottage cheese, tofu in cooking.
Meat	Leaner cuts, grill don't fry, vegetarian savouries, e.g. tofu.

manufactured by the liver and intestines from fats, proteins and sugars in the diet. There are also other foods and drinks which contrive to exert their influence on the heart through the cholesterol metabolism, as well as in other ways.

Sugar

Sugar is another of those foods which tends to find its way into our diet by many devious routes. Quite apart from its use as a sweetener, it appears in some savoury foods, such as baked beans

The problem with sugar lies mainly in the refining process which makes a far more concentrated product than our digestive systems were ever made to cope with. To produce the amount of sugar some people consume in a week in tea and coffee alone would require 16 pounds of sugar beet. If they were prepared to chew their way through raw beet there would no problem! One heaped teaspoonful of sugar is equivalent to the amount in an apple but because of the cellulose fibre of the apple the sugar is released to the blood only slowly.

Diabetes

It is well known that diabetics are at greater risk of heart-disease. People who develop diabetes in middle age are often those who have had an excessively sweet-toothed youth. A constant over-stimulation of the pancreas, which produces insulin to break down sugar for energy, eventually exhausts it. But the excessively high sugar levels also raise the blood cholesterol. It has been found that by avoiding foods which contain sugar, corn sweetener, fructose, sucrose and glucose, cholesterol levels can be reduced by 20-30%.

Reducing sugar consumption is, therefore, another essential step for the angina patient. Even honey must be used only sparingly. Fructose (fruit sugar) is also more slowly absorbed than most other types and it may be suitable for cooking. Fresh or dried fruits, and the sugar-free fruit preserves now available from health food stores may satisfy your need for something sweet. Artificial sweeteners are not recommended as in some cases they are suspected of being carcinogenic (cancer causing).

Paradoxically, consumption of large amounts of sweet foods can also engender chronic fatigue. The over-irritated pancreas repeatedly pushes out more insulin than may be required which causes the blood-sugar level to fall below the normal needed to nourish the nervous system and the body generally. It is during these hypoglycaemic (low blood-sugar) phases that the individual becomes tired, tense, and irritable — in fact, highly vulnerable to stress and excessive arousal. And we know that stress elevates the cholesterol levels and induces angina attacks.

Protein

Protein foods are more sustaining in the long run because the body converts them to energy only slowly. You may, however, have to review the sources of protein in your diet.

In general animal protein, such as meat and dairy produce, creates more cholesterol than vegetable protein. This is particularly true of domestic beef and poultry which has been intensively reared. The amount of fat on the unexercised yard or battery-bred steer and chicken is significantly greater than their wild counterparts.

Dairy proteins, such as cheese and eggs, also provide more cholesterol than we need. An egg yolk contains 300mg cholesterol whilst our bodies only manufacture 100-200mg per day. But it may not be wise to exclude eggs entirely.

They are a valuable and convenient source of protein and contain other important nutrients, such as zinc and lecithin, which help the body to create energy and mobilize fats. A couple of eggs twice a week should meet the body's needs provided your cholesterol levels are not high.

First class protein
Vegetables, grains, and pulses provide considerable amounts of protein. Protein foods are made up of amino acids, some of which are termed essential, because the body cannot synthesize them from other foods. This means that they must be provided in the diet on an almost daily basis. It is generally supposed that only animal proteins can provide these and they are, therefore, termed 'first class proteins', but nutritionists now know that proper combining of vegetable protein can give the body all its requirements without the saturated fats.

According to nutritional biochemist Dr Jeffrey Bland, of the Linus Pauling Institute, Palo Alto, California, the amino acid requirements can be balanced by taking two parts grains (rice, millet, buckwheat, etc.) to one part legumes (beans, lentils, etc). Vegetable protein has a lower ratio of the amino acids lysine to arginine than does meat. When the lysine to arginine ratio is high the liver tends to produce more cholesterol.

Alternative proteins
You may add variety to your protein intake by introducing some of the more unusual foods from Europe and the Far East:

Tahini is a sesame seed paste which may be added to muesli or fruit salad, incorporated in sauces and dressings, and used as a spread. Sesame seeds are high in polyunsaturated fats.

Tofu, or soya bean curd, is a most versatile food: It can be used in stews or other savoury dishes, is an agreeable alternative to cheese in flans, can be blended in salad dressings, and can be made into a mousse (flavoured with fruit juice) as a dessert.

Sunflower seeds are a complete protein food, and can make an excellent light snack between meals or be added to salads and muesli.

Coffee and tea

The caffeine in tea, coffee and other beverages, such as canned or bottled cola drinks, is another stimulant that gives the body a lift which it rapidly loses. Coffee is a real problem drink for angina patients. The caffeine stimulates the nervous system, inducing general arousal and sometimes palpitations or irregularity of the heartbeat, and it irritates the stomach causing indigestion. Many people also find that it prevents them sleeping satisfactorily.

There is still some debate over the effect of coffee on cholesterol levels. A study of 1,228 women and 923 men who were regular coffee drinkers, indicated, over a period of four years, that it was associated with increases in total blood fats and LDL cholesterol. In a Norwegian trial 33 men with high blood cholesterol followed different patterns of coffee consumption. The first group continued normal coffee intake. A second group stopped coffee altogether, whilst the third stopped for five weeks then drank boiled or filtered coffee. The cholesterol level was significantly reduced in all the abstainers during the first five weeks. Coffee will also aggravate hypoglycaemia and lead to chronic fatigue. It also increases the urinary output of potassium thereby reducing the body's reserves of that important mineral.

Any angina subject would be wise to keep off coffee, and even to be cautious with decaffeinated varieties. There is evidence that other solids remaining in the coffee after decaffeination can also be hazardous. Strong tea also contains tannin which is a digestive irritant. Drink the weaker teas, or better still use one of the many varieties of herbal teas or coffee substitutes, such as those made on the continent with barley, figs and chicory.

Alcohol

Alcoholic beverages are a mixed blessing for angina cases. It is very much a matter of moderation. When 12 healthy volunteers drank half a bottle of wine per day for 6 weeks their plasma HDL increased; during a 6 week period of abstention it fell. Moderate alcohol intake, therefore, seems to be beneficial in maintaining a healthier balance of blood fats.

Alcohol also aids relaxation and dilates the blood vessels but in these benefits lie its potential dangers. It would be wrong to rely on alcohol to alleviate the tensions induced by an over-pressured lifestyle, a caution which applies to other 'crutches', such as tranquillizers, which do not rectify the real cause of the trouble. The inevitable trend with such short term methods of relief is to require more and more.

Larger amounts of alcohol have been found to increase the blood fats. Increased alcohol also reduces the muscular efficiency of the heart, especially if it is taken before exercise. Generally, alcohol reduces the efficiency of the stomach and liver enzymes and interferes with the absorption of certain vitamins. It also increases the loss of potassium in the urine.

It is, therefore, advisable to restrict your alcohol intake to a glass or two of wine per day with beers and spirits no more than once or twice a week on more special occasions.

Salt

Salt has been such an integral part of man's diet for thousands of years that it is surprising to find that it has an undesirable effect on health. Excessive sodium intake has been correlated with high blood-pressure and heart problems. Although the average diet contains large amounts of salt it may be the relative shortage of potassium which accounts for the prevalence of problems in the twentieth century. Potassium is essential for healthy heart function but also acts as a balancing mineral to sodium in the diet. In ancient times sea salt was probably in more common currency. Sea salt gives a more natural balance of the minerals than refined rock salt.

A Swedish trial, reported in the *Journal of Clinical Science* (Volume 6, No. 5, 1984) tested the effect on 37 men, with normal blood-pressures, of 12g salt daily for 4 weeks in addition to their normal intake. The systolic blood-pressure and the weight increased significantly in those men with a family history of blood-pressure as well as those without.

The high salt content of the modern diet derives mainly from processed foods which contain more sodium and less potassium than unprocessed foods. A Canadian study suggested that 60% of sodium in the diet comes from processing of food by industry and in the home.

A restriction of salt intake was one of the recommendations of the COMA report. Don't add extra salt to food and confine yourself to a little sea salt in cooking. Use herbs to give flavour to your food if necessary, but, when you cut out salt and condiments, you will find, after a few weeks, that your taste buds will come back to life and appreciate the real flavour of the vegetables.

Fibre

Although roughage — the relatively indigestible cellulose and fibrous material in our diet — does not, in itself, have much nutritional value, it is important for the maintenance of good health. The bulk it provides in the intestines, for example, ensures regular bowel function and proper elimination of surplus cholesterol. It is also a valuable regulator of fluids encouraging their elimination. Fibre provides an extra surface area for the bacteria which are such important inhabitants of our intestines. Intestinal bacteria help us to assimilate certain vitamins of the B complex.

A well-balanced diet with wholegrains, pulses,

fresh fruit and vegetables will normally contain plenty of fibre. If you do take any extra in the form of bran, for example, it is most important to have other high-fibre foods such as wholemeal bread, since the phytic acid in bran, which is not digested by yeast in the way that it is in bread, may obstruct the absorption of certain nutrients, particularly iron. Oat bran fibre is the best form to use since it is less indigestible than wheat bran.

Preparing food

A reasonable proportion of your daily food intake should consist of raw material — salads and fresh fruit. The vitamin and mineral content of raw foods is higher and they have the greatest energy potential. Other foods, such as grains and some vegetables are more easily digested when cooked, but cooking should be done in such a way as to minimize the destruction of essential nutrients.

Conservative cooking

The method of conservative cooking of vegetables, for example, uses a small amount of water in which they are simmered until just tender, rather than boiling them to a tasteless sog.

Experiments have shown that heat-damaged cholesterol is more conducive to heart-disease. Frying is particularly unsuitable because the fat is rapidly oxidised. Frying an egg is, therefore, more hazardous than soft boiling or poaching.

All vegetable oils should be cooked for only a short time since prolonged heating, or reheating, encourages their conversion to substances which initiate increased cholesterol levels.

Cooking utensils
The type of cooking utensils you use may also have an adverse effect on nutritional status. Aluminium saucepans should never be used for fruit and vegetables since the acids erode the surface and take up traces of the metal. Aluminium is a toxic metal which can interfere with the function of digestive enzymes and impair the assimilation of some vitamins and minerals. The most suitable utensils are those made of stainless steel.

The Basic Diet
By adopting a diet in which the majority of foods are as near as possible to their natural state you will automatically institute the recommendations to limit sugar, fats and salt and to increase the fibre. This has, for some years, been referred to as a wholefood diet and, more recently, in some circles as a 'stone age' diet because it is free of the processes and embellishments of modernity.

The menu given on page 98 suggests various alternatives for each time of day as an example of the types of foods and drinks which you may have. It is by no means mandatory to eat as this suggests, and an occasional meal containing some of the more hazardous foods will do no harm provided your general nutritional standard is high.

BASIC HEALTH DIET

Morning
One of the following may be taken. Fresh fruit in season, dried fruit (e.g. apricots, prunes), baked or puréed apple with raisins, muesli, wholemeal or rye bread toasted or fresh, with unsalted butter or sunflower margarine and honey or savoury spread. If a drink is required, a glass of pure unsweetened fruit juice, China or herb tea, coffee substitute or other hot drink as described below may be taken.

Mid-Morning
If a drink is required use pure unsweetened fruit juice, China tea, good quality decaffeinated coffee or coffee substitute. Low-sodium yeast extracts or other savouries, such as miso, may be made into a warm drink by mixing one teaspoonful with a cup of hot water. If a snack is required use sunflower seeds, nuts or biscuits made with wholegrains.

Midday Meal
Mixed vegetable salad consisting of selection of lettuce, tomatoes, Chinese leaves, cress, celery, white cabbage, carrots, radishes, cucumber, onions, beetroot (raw and grated), chicory, garlic, endive, to which may be added raisins or dates, cottage or goat's milk cheese, milled nuts, and a dressing of cider vinegar and yogurt or tofu. Wholemeal or rye bread or wholemeal biscuits with savoury spread.
OR warm savoury dish (egg, lean meat, fish, cheese, or nut or other savoury) with

conservatively cooked vegetables and baked jacket potato, or cereal grains.

For dessert: soaked dried fruit, baked apple, fresh fruit, muesli, yogurt, soured milk, carageen or natural fruit jelly.

Mid-Afternoon

As mid-morning.

Evening Meal

Alternative to midday meal. The salad meal may be taken at midday or in the evening according to preference and convenience. It is desirable to have one raw salad meal per day throughout the year. Dessert — as for lunch.

Before Retiring

If a drink is required choose from the list given above. It is preferable not to eat unless otherwise directed.

*   *   *   *   *   *   *   *

Nutritional Supplements

The orthodox nutritional viewpoint argues that the modern mixed diet meets all our nutritional requirements. The basic diet should provide all the essential nutrients for good health but not everyone has the capacity to use them. Furthermore people's needs vary enormously and the recommended dietary allowances (RDAs) which suggest how much of each nutrient we require each day are often inadequate. These figures are worked out from the average intake of a 'normal healthy group of people', but in this context 'healthy' means only absence of disease and not positive well-being.

Also few people are 'average'. Under certain circumstances larger amounts of some vitamins and minerals are necessary to promote functions which have deteriorated. At times of stress, or during infections, the body's needs for vitamins B and C, for example, may be considerably greater than the RDAs.

A case could be argued for taking almost every supplement under the sun, since all nutrients must affect heart function directly or indirectly but there are undoubtedly some which can be particularly helpful when taken in the context of a sensible wholefood diet.

Supplements are just that — an addition to a properly balanced diet, for the different nutrients are interdependent in a positive and negative way. Vitamin B_6, for example, is necessary to prevent atherosclerosis, but cannot be effectively assimilated without other vitamins of the B complex group. The toxic metal Cadmium, present especially in cigarette smoke, refined food and the water of some areas, antagonizes calcium and magnesium in the body. It can also contribute to high blood-pressure where the calcium, magnesium, and zinc levels are low.

Your levels of the important vitamins and minerals can be increased by eating more of the foods in which they are richest (see Tables 2 and 3) but supplements are also available from health food stores who market preparations made from natural sources that are more biologically active than the synthesized types imitated by the chemist.

Table 2: Food Sources of Important Vitamins

Vitamin	Obtained from
A	liver, eggs, carrots, swedes.
B Complex	Brewer's yeast, liver, wholegrain cereals. Yogurt encourages intestinal bacteria which synthesize vitamin B.
C	most fresh fruit and vegetables especially citrus fruit, green peppers, watercress, sprouted alfalfa seeds, broccoli, Brazil nuts.
E	vegetable oils, eggs, wheatgerm, wholegrains, leafy vegetables, sweet potatoes, raw seeds and nuts, soya beans.

Magnesium is essential to reduce cramping of muscles. It works with calcium to maintain normal contractility of the heart muscle. It also helps the absorption and metabolism of other minerals such as calcium, phosphorus, and potassium, as well as vitamins C and E.

Calcium and magnesium are available in a balanced form in the natural dietary supplement Dolomite available from most health food stores.

Potassium encourages the excretion of sodium, maintaining a correct balance for normal heartbeat. Potassium is an important nutrient

Table 3: Food Sources of Important Minerals

Mineral	Obtained from
Calcium	soya milk, tahini (sesame seeds), sunflower seeds, Ricotta cheese, yogurt.
Iron	liver, green leafy vegetables especially watercress.
Magnesium	fresh green vegetables, sunflower seeds, tahini, soya beans, almonds.
Potassium	green leafy vegetables, root vegetables especially potatoes, wholegrains, sunflower seeds, bananas.
Zinc	wholegrains, especially oatmeal, liver, egg yolk.

in the function of nervous conductivity, particularly of those nerve impulses regulating heart rate. Inadequate potassium can also impair normal sleeping patterns.

Calcium is a poorly absorbed mineral at the best of times and is particularly dependent on adequate stomach acids and other minerals, such as magnesium, with which it is found in Dolomite supplement. It works with potassium and magnesium in the body to maintain healthy function of the nervous sytem and heart as well as aiding good sleep. Calcium is also essential to the passage of nutrients through cell walls.

Apart from Dolomite, non-vegetarians can use bone meal as a supplement of calcium. Another valuable source is the eggshell! Dr Carl Pfeiffer in his book *Mental and Elemental Nutrients*, suggests standing an egg in cider vinegar for 24 hours to soften the shell then throwing the whole egg into a blender to make an egg nog. The cider vinegar will also assist the stomach acid.

Zinc is a trace element commonly lacking in the diet and its absorption is easily suppressed by excessive calcium. Another trace element which antagonizes zinc is copper, levels of which tend to be high in womens' pre-menstrual phase and after ingestion of refined foods. Copper is not all bad — we also need it in small amounts — but deficiency of zinc may allow it to cause problems.

Zinc deficiency, indicated in part by stretch marks, and white spots on the fingernails, is best made up by foods in which it is rich, or a compound mineral supplement, as it is mutually interdependent with vitamin B_6 and other nutrients. Excessive zinc, however, can reduce the HDL cholesterol — the type we need — so don't overdo supplements.

Vitamin B is a whole range of vitamins, all of which play an important role in energy production. Choline, biotin, pangamic acid, inositol, and B_{12} are all vitamins of the B complex which prevent accumulation of fat in the liver. Our intestinal bacteria are an important source of B vitamins, so antibiotics, which destroy them, may cause relative deficiency, as will alcohol and sleeping tablets. It is best to use a B complex supplement, although added amounts of B_6, choline, and biotin may also be advisable.

Vitamin C intake often needs supplementing because it is so readily lost from foods by processing and cooking and from the body by stress, smoking, drugs, and inhalation of fumes. It has important interactions with many other nutrients such a calcium, magnesium, vitamin B and vitamin E, with which it helps to conserve oxygen so essential for the angina victim.

Vitamin C helps to reduce the fragility of the blood capillaries. When the vessels break down clotting is more liable to occur. A supplement of 200mg vitamin C per day was found to reduce cholesterol levels when they were high but had no effect when they were at, or near, normal levels. This shows that the body uses these nutrients only to restore and maintain normality. Vitamin C also prevents conversion of the fatty acid arachidonic acid to a hormone which increases the adhesiveness of platelets.

Use the supplemental form of vitamin C known as bioflavonoids, which is a compound with vitamin P, another protector of blood vessels found with the C in nature.

Vitamin E is essential in a diet which includes large amounts of polyunsaturated fats (vegetable oils, fish, margarine) because it prevents their oxidation and reduces the rate at which they go rancid. These foods increase the need for vitamin E but also contain it themselves.

Vitamin E, like thyroid hormone, is an oestrogen antagonist and in women with a deficiency of thyroid function the higher levels of oestrogen, especially in the pre-menstrual phase, can increase the risk of heart damage and thrombosis. Vitamin E is, therefore, protective and because of its anti-oxidant effect is a valuable promoter of normal coronary artery function.

Vitamin E should be supplemented in low doses to start with, especially if the blood-pressure is elevated. Commence with 100-200IU increasing to 400-600IU if blood-pressure is normal.

Kelp is a seaweed which is a rich natural source of iodine necessary for healthy thyroid function. It also contains vitamins of the B complex, vitamin E, calcium and magnesium, so may be used in tablet form available from health food stores, or powdered as a salt substitute.

Lecithin occurs naturally in eggs and soya products as well as vegetable oils. It helps to emulsify fats but may also be taken as a supplement in the form of capsules available from your health food store.

Quantities

You will notice that I have made few recommendations as to the amounts of different nutrients or supplements to take each day. In the case of daily food intake it is time consuming and boring to have to concern oneself with quantities and the counting of calories. Individual needs vary so much and common sense servings of most natural foods will provide adequate nourishment in many cases. Remember that quality is far more important than quantity.

Where vitamin and mineral supplements are concerned the best rule-of-thumb is to use the maximum dose recommended by the manufacturers. This will generally ensure at least the recommended daily requirement and larger amounts may be taken by eating more of the foods which are rich in the important nutrients such as vitamin B, potassium and vitamin C.

Because of the complexities of nutrient interactions a compound or multimineral supplement is a good idea, but do use the type prepared from natural ingredients available from your health food store.

A Final Word About Food

In managing angina it is probably more important to avoid anxiety than additives, fats, and sugar, so, by all means make an effort to reform your diet but don't let it become an obsession. An odd rich meal is unlikely to do serious harm especially if enjoyed in an atmosphere of conviviality.

Avoid being over-full; it is better to eat small amounts more frequently than to have occasional large blow-outs. Above all try to ensure that all meals are eaten with enjoyment and equanimity.

6.

Seeking Professional Help

An important aspect of helping yourself with the management of angina is being able to recognize, and act upon, the need to obtain professional help. The good thing about *NEW SELF-HELP FOR ANGINA* is that the range of professional skills available is now greater than ever before.

It is characteristic of the angina-prone Type A personality, to be stoic and battle on regardless of the warning signs the body offers. 'I can't allow a bit of chest pain to stop me now! There isn't time to go running to my doctor', is the usual stubborn attitude.

If you experience chest pain, especially on or after exertion or extra stress, you should see your doctor. A timely examination and appropriate care can be life-saving. If a further investigation is necessary a doctor has access to the best technical resources to determine the state of your heart and arteries. You then have a number of other options in complementary medical systems which offer advice and treatment on various aspects of your health, as well as a number of peripheral aids, such as yoga and exercise classes, relaxation, and massage.

In this brief survey I have tried to give some idea of the principle resources available to you and the type of advice and the treatment they might give.

Medicine and Surgery

When you consult your doctor his first objective will be to determine the cause of your chest pains. Apart from a general examination, which will include a check of heart, lungs, and blood-pressure, he may carry out, or refer you for, an electrocardiograph (ECG) which records the rhythms of the heart. The ECG may not always show any abnormality unless it is done while the heart is actually misbehaving. A mild heart attack can leave no electrical signs after it has taken place and the heart has got back to relative normality, but the ECG may provide useful information as to the balance of the heart's contractions.

After there has been some damage to the heart muscle it does leave biochemical changes which can be revealed by blood tests. Certain enzymes are released by the damaged muscles and serve as a guide to the intensity of the problem. Blood tests can also detect the levels of cholesterol and the different types of fats, though, of course, in many cases of angina these may be perfectly normal. Your doctor may try to give relief of the immediate discomfort by prescribing drugs, perhaps glyceryl trinitrate, for the alleviation of the anginal attacks, and a tranquillizer if it seems that stress is playing some part in the onset of the problem. Other drugs are also commonly prescribed, such as a group known as the beta-blockers, which are designed to slow down the rate of conduction of the nervous impulses by blocking, to some degree, the biochemical changes that take place between the nerve endings. These drugs also tend to slow the rate of the heartbeat.

You may also be advised to reorganize your life to reduce the amount of arousal to which you subject yourself. If these measures don't succeed in reducing the discomfort you experience you may well be referred for further investigations. If the blood fats are above normal levels there is a probability of a furring up of the coronary arteries and a heart specialist (cardiologist) might carry out further investigations to decide whether the arteries are so obstructed as to need by-pass surgery.

The coronary artery by-pass operation is now performed in many thousands of cases per year. One or more veins are removed from the thigh and grafted into the heart to by-pass the narrowed or obstructed artery. This restores a fuller flow of blood to the heart muscle.

Seventy to ninety per cent of coronary by-pass cases improve, but, according to the Canadian heart specialist, Dr Wilfrid Shute, so too did 60% of cases in whom an incision was made under anaesthetic and then sewn up again without touching the heart! A significant placebo effect has also been achieved with dummy tablets when compared with drugs used for the relief of angina.

All the skills of surgery and the power of drugs (or placebos!) do not rectify the real causes of angina, which, as you will now be aware, operate at many different levels. Relaxing the arteries with a chemical and replacing them with grafted veins takes care of the mechanical aspects of angina but it doesn't do anything to help the individual to learn to live more effectively and to cope with life. This is where a number of the complementary medical systems can offer constructive help.

Naturopathic Medicine

The naturopath carries out similar investigations to the doctor. His examination of heart, lungs, blood-pressure, and interpretation of blood tests (which will not be needed if your doctor has already had them done) will be combined with investigations of the spine and muscular systems, inspection of the iris of the eyes (irisdiagnosis) and enquiries about lifestyle and dietary habits in order to build up a picture of your potential for health and recovery.

Naturopathic medicine recognizes that health depends equally upon our emotional, structural and biochemical functions, all of which must be well integrated for us to remain well. Naturopathic treatment and advice may, therefore, range widely from counselling and relaxation techniques for the anxious or over-tense individual, to dietary advice and applied nutrition — the use of controlled intake and vitamin or mineral supplements — for the management of such problems as high blood-pressure. Programmes of fasting on raw juices, or raw fruit and vegetable diets, under the supervision of naturopaths, have proved effective in the reduction of some types of blood-pressure and congestion of the heart or lungs. Many naturopaths also practise osteopathy and use a specialized form of muscle tension release, known as the neuromuscular technique, which can greatly aid relaxation of the chest and back muscles. In short, the naturopath is concerned with the health of the whole person and can offer valuable specialist guidance to supplement that of your doctor in promoting general well-being.

Medical Herbalism

Various types of herbal preparations which can help with problems allied to angina, such as insomnia and constipation, are available from health food stores. Of particular value, for example, are garlic tablets or capsules (the former are marginally more effective). Garlic has been found to be an effective anticoagulant, reducing the cholesterol levels. Three or four tablets swallowed last thing at night pose few social problems!

More specialized advice on the use of herbal medicines is obtainable from a consulting medical herbalist. The medical herbalist is trained to carry out a full examination along similar lines to that of a doctor or naturopath, and, on the basis of this, he may decide upon appropriate combinations of herbs which are given either as liquid extracts, tinctures or dried herbs from which you may make infusions.

The herbal practitioner may choose herbs to give tone and support to the heart and circulation, such as Hawthorn and the Night-blooming Cactus, and others which nourish and strengthen the nerves, such as Skullcap and Passion flower. The herbalist is skilled in the selection of appropriate plants in the correct dosage and combination for the management of your condition.

Homoeopathy

Another method of prescribing uses infinitesimal proportions of plant extracts and minerals to support the functions of the heart and circulation. The homoeopath also makes a careful assessment of the whole patient, paying as much attention to the mental and emotional influences (and such idiosyncracies as taste preferences, thirst, changes of appetite, and susceptibility to weather change) as to physical signs and symptoms.

Medicines are prepared by a series of dilutions to various degrees by either decimal or centesimal stages known as potencies. The 1x potency (decimal) is one part of the medicine or tincture in nine parts of distilled water and the 1c (centesimal) is one part of the medicine or tincture in 99 parts of water. The 2c potency is made by mixing one part of the 1c solution with 99 parts of water, and so on. The greater dilutions, above 6c, contain no measurable trace of the original medicine but their therapeutic power is greater. This is believed to be effected because of some vibrational frequency which the appropriate remedy and potency has with the patient and his illness. It is, therefore, most important for the correct single remedy to be selected for the individual although, in the lower potencies, remedies can be effectively combined.

Homoeopathy is a valuable and safe form of treatment for many acute disorders, such as colds, 'flu, and gastroenteritis, being infinitely preferable to antibiotics, which destroy the friendly intestinal bacteria. Practitioners can also prescribe remedies to ease the angina condition but, because of the individuality of approach, they would probably be different for two people with similar symptoms.

Acupuncture

Acupuncture is part of a system of medicine originated in China several thousand years ago, in which the human body is seen as a unified organism made up of interdependent systems which are subject to the internal influences of the emotions fear, anger, joy, and so on, and the external factors of the environment, such as food, climate and physical phenomena. Using fine needles, a burning herb or mild electrical stimulation, the acupuncturist treats points on the body surface which are believed to be interconnected by channels, known as meridians, which have connections with the organs of the body. This treatment may sound rather alarming but is, in fact, very gentle, virtually pain free and, invariably, most relaxing.

Traditional Chinese medicine is based on the principle that there exists in the body a vital energy, known as *chi*, which maintains a balance between its polarities of *yin*, the cool, dark, expansive principle, and *yang*, the hot, light, contractile principle. Allowing for the natural predominance in the male of the yang principle and the female of the yin principle there should, in normal health, be a balance between the two. The easily aroused angina patient with high blood-pressure, for example, would be considered to be excessively yang but could, eventually, through exhaustion of reserves, become deficient in energy.

The practitioner of traditional Chinese acupuncture assesses the requirements of his patient by taking a careful case history, doing a general examination, and paying particular attention to the quality of the pulses on each wrist and signs revealed by observation of the tongue. This information is then integrated to select the appropriate points and method of treatment.

Modern research has shown that the stimulation of certain acupuncture points promotes the release of pain-relieving hormones by the brain. Acupuncture can also bring about other biochemical changes in the body, such as an increase of natural cortisone secretion, which relieves the pain and stiffness of rheumatism and arthritis, and it has also been shown to promote the functions of the immune system, which helps the body to fight infections. These discoveries cannot yet account for all the benefits of acupuncture and most practitioners find that a thorough understanding of the traditional concepts and application of their treatments on the basis of these, rather than simply using points as pain relievers, brings better all-round results.

As an angina sufferer you may find

acupuncture a valuable treatment to aid relaxation and reintegrate many other functions of the body, such as the musculoskeletal system and digestion, to aid in coping more effectively with your complaint.

Osteopathy

A common discomfort for the person with angina is a feeling of restriction around the neck, shoulders and upper back. This often exaggerates the sensation of constriction in the chest. Even when free from angina attacks there can be a general stiffness and limitation of movement in these areas which keeps one that much closer to the threshold of pain and may also lead to problems such as headaches, numbness, or tingling of the hands and fingers, and arthritic degeneration in the bones of the neck.

Osteopathy is a system of medicine which concentrates on reintegrating the joints and muscles of the body, particularly those of the head, neck and back, to restore better mobility. Restrictions in the movement of back joints, apart from causing local discomfort, can impair the functions of nerves which pass out between the bones, from the spinal cord, to supply all the organs of the body. These limitations of mobility can also interfere with the normal flow of blood. The objective of the osteopath is to remove such obstacles to promote healthy function.

The osteopath will usually carry out a general examination because he needs to assess the state of your musculo-skeletal system in the context of your total health. In the examination of the spine he will feel carefully for the position and range of movement of the individual bones and the condition of the muscles and ligaments. This process of exploratory diagnosis becomes the treatment as stiffened and contracted muscle fibres are stretched and ligament tone is rebalanced by special soft tissue massage techniques which most osteopaths use. Joints are gently eased or more specific manipulative procedures are used to release those which are locked in limited mobility.

Some osteopaths practise a gentle form of reintegration of the bones of the skull, known as Cranial Osteopathy. The subtle rhythmical movements of the cranial bones work in harmony with the rest of the spinal column to promote the flow of cerebrospinal fluid which nourishes the brain and nervous system.

Chiropractic

Chiropractic is another system of structural reintegration which differs from osteopathy primarily in the techniques used to achieve this. The chiropractor's main objective is to restore nervous equilibrium by correction of displacements of the spinal vertebrae. Many chiropractors now use a sophisticated system of muscle reflex testing known as Applied Kinesiology, by which it is possible to detect the functional imbalances of the rest of the body as well as some dietary sensitivities and deficiencies.

Additional Aids

There are various other treatments which,

although they are not complete medical systems, can be of great benefit to the person with angina. If there are therapists near you it is worth trying some of the following.

Alexander Technique

Not so much a therapy as a system of teaching postural awareness and encouraging better 'use of the self' as Matthias Alexander, the originator of the system, called it. By lying, sitting, standing, and walking more effectively you will gain better poise and reduce both physical and mental tensions.

Teachers of the Alexander Technique undergo a lengthy and rigorous training and give careful instruction to develop your awareness of faulty habit patterns and cultivate newer healthy ones. To be effective the process takes some months but it is a worthwhile and valuable aid to relaxation and comfortable movement for people with angina.

Autogenic training

This is one of a number of methods of learning to relax and let go physically. The subject is trained to be in a relaxed state and concentrate on release of tensions in different parts of the body. With practice this method can reduce the level of arousal (see Relaxation Routine on pages 67–9).

Massage

There are many forms of massage now practised, some of a more general nature and some based on the use of energy points and reflex zones. The latter, such as Shiatzu, and Do In, a Japanese system of self massage, work on reintegration of the body's energy system.

Nearly all forms of massage are valuable aids to physical relaxation and general well-being for the angina patient.

Reflexology
This is a specialized technique of foot massage originated by Eunice Ingham in the USA. Reflex zones on the feet are gently massaged to improve the energy and function of the whole body. The feet, our contact with the energy of the earth, are rich in nerve endings and are an important influence on our health.

Foot reflexology is comforting and calming for the over-aroused or exhausted angina victim. Choose an experienced operator as overlong work on sensitive feet can be too stimulating to the nervous system and lead to exhaustion.

Bach flower remedies
Though really an extension of the homoeopathic system, the Bach flower remedies are mentioned here because they are easy to select and use for yourself. Dr Edward Bach was a physician who discovered in the 1930s that a number of plant essences, prepared by distillation in sunlight, had the properties of assisting people with emotional states, such as fear, anxiety, impatience or depression. There are 37 different Bach remedies suitable for many states of mind and they meet the needs of angina patients particularly well. The following few examples will illustrate why:

Remedy	Indications
Aspen	Fear, apprehension, terror on waking, fear of death.
Elm	Feelings of being over-whelmed by responsibility.
Honeysuckle	Looking back with regret, bereavement, failure in business.
Hornbeam	Mental fatigue.
Impatiens	Impatience, tension.
Olive	Overworking, hiding tiredness.
Rockwater	Hard taskmasters to themselves, tension.
White chestnut	Insomnia, mental preoccupation
Rescue remedy	A combination of 5 flower remedies for shock, panic situations, fear.

Two drops of one or more of the selected remedies are prepared in a small bottle of plain water. A few drops of this solution are then placed in any drinks throughout the day. Stock bottles of each remedy are available from homoeopathic pharmacies, or from The Dr Edward Bach Healing Centre, Mount Vernon, Sotwell, Wallingford, Oxon, OX10 0PZ. Send a stamped addressed envelope to them for further information and instructions.

A few drops of Rescue Remedy placed on or under the tongue can be very helpful during an angina attack.

Further Reading

General

B.M.A. Book of Executive Health (Times Books)
The Heart Attack Recovery Book Elizabeth Wilde McCormick (Coventure)
Natural Medicine Brian Inglis (Koestler Foundation)
Will to be Well Neville Hodgkinson (Hutchinson)

Exercise and Relaxation

How to Meditate Lawrence Le Shan (Thorsons)
Yoga Self Taught André van Lysebeth (Allen & Unwin)
Your Complete Stress-Proofing Programme Leon Chaitow (Thorsons)
Your Personal Health Programme Jeffrey Bland (Thorsons)

Food and Health

Diets to Help Control Cholesterol Roger Newman Turner (Thorsons)
Diets to Help Heart Disorders Roger Newman Turner (Thorsons)
Diets to Help Hypertension Clifford Quick (Thorsons)

Tofu Cookery Louise Hagler (Thorsons)
Your Health Under Siege Jeffrey Bland (Thorsons)

Further Help

Acupuncture George Lewith (Thorsons)
The Alternative Health Guide Brian Inglis & Ruth West (Michael Joseph)
Dictionary of the Bach Flower Remedies Dr Edward Bach Healing Centre (see page 123)
Homoeopathy Keith Scott & Linda McCourt (Thorsons)
Naturopathic Medicine Roger Newman Turner (Thorsons)
Ostcopathy Leon Chaitow (Thorsons)

Useful Addresses

PROFESSIONAL ASSOCIATIONS

Most associations publish a directory of qualified practitioners and literature explaining more about the system of medicine they represent.

British Naturopathic and Osteopathic Association

Frazer House, 6 Netherhall Gardens, London, NW3 5RR. (01 435 8728) (literature, directory and speakers)

General Council and Register of Osteopaths

1-4 Suffolk Street, London SW1Y 4HG. (01 839 2060) (literature and directory)

Society of Osteopaths

12 College Road, Eastbourne, East Sussex. (0323 638606) (directory and information)

College of Osteopaths' Practitioners Association

110 Thorkill Road, Thames Ditton, Surrey, KT7 OUW. (01 398 3308)

Cranial Osteopathic Association
Hatton House, Church Lane, Cheshunt, Herts, EN8 ODW. (0992 32085)

British Chiropractic Association
5 First Avenue, Chelmsford, Essex, CM1 IRX. (0245 358487) (literature and directory)

British Acupuncture Association
34 Alderney Street, London, SW1V 4EU. (01 834 1012/3353) (handbook, directory and speakers)

Register of Traditional Chinese Medicine
7a Thorndean Street, London, SW18. (01 947 1879)

Traditional Acupuncture Society
11 Grange Park, Stratford-upon-Avon, Warwickshire, CV37 6XH. (0789 298798)

International Register of Oriental Medicine
Green Hedges House, Green Hedges Avenue, East Grinstead, Sussex, RH19 1DZ. (0342 28567)

National Institute of Medical Herbalists
41 Hatherley Road, Winchester, Hampshire, SO22 6RR. (0962 68776)

Dr Edward Bach Centre
Mount Vernon, Sotwell, Wallingford, Oxon, OX10 OPZ. (0491 39489)

British Homoeopathic Association
27a Devonshire Street, London, W1N 1RJ. (01 935 2163) (literature and lists of medical homoeopaths)

Society of Homoeopaths
2a Bedford Place, Southampton, SO1 2BY. (0703 222364) (qualified non-doctor homoeopaths)

The Bayly School of Reflexology
Monks Orchard, Whitbourne, Worcester, WR6 5RB. (0886 21207)

International Institute of Reflexology
PO Box 34, Harlow, Essex, CM17 OLT. (0279 29060)

HEALTH AND SELF-HELP ORGANIZATIONS

The Nutrition Foundation
24 Harcourt House, 19 Cavendish Square, London, W1M 9AB.

Action on Smoking and Health (ASH)
27-35 Mortimer Street, London, W1N 7RJ. (01 637 9843) (literature giving advice on the dangers of smoking and how to give it up)

Health Education Council
78 New Oxford Street, London, WC1A 1AH. (01 637 1881) (literature on many health topics; can also provide speakers on health education)

Chest, Heart and Stroke Assocation

Tavistock House, Tavistock Square, London, WC1H 9JE. (01 387 3012) (information and welfare service)

Alcoholics Anonymous

11 Redcliffe Gardens, London, SW10 9BG. (01 834 8202) (advice and support for alcoholics and their families)

City Gym (Alistair Murray)

New Union Street, London, EC2Y 9BU. (01 628 0786) (Cardiac Rehabiliation Clinics and a fitness gymnasium)

INDEX

abdominal breathing, 76–7

acupuncture, 113

adrenalin, 20, 34, 75

aggression, 28

alcohol, 93–4

Alexander Technique, 117

amino acids, 91

angina, false, 16

angina, symptoms of, 22–3

arginine, 91

atheroma, 18

atherosclerosis, 18, 20, 27, 100

attitude, change of, 54

autogenic training, 66, 117

Bach flower remedies, 118

beta-blockers, 12, 72, 109

beverages, 21

biofeedback methods, 65

blood-pressure, high, 18

breathing, abdominal, 76–7

by-pass operations, 12, 21, 109

Cadmium, 100

caffeine, 21, 61, 92

calcium, 62, 100, 101, 102

carbon dioxide, 20, 25

catecholamines, 20

Catford, Professor John, 11

changes in life, impact of, 39–41

chiropractic, 116

cholesterol, 27, 87

climate, 41

coffee, 21, 61, 92–3

Committee on Medical Aspects of Food Policy (COMA), the, 81

commuting, 51–2

competitiveness, 28

conservative cooking, 96–7

cooking utensils, 97

coronary arteries, 11, 16, 18, 21, 24, 26, 45, 57

coronary thrombosis, 24

cortisol, 34

cranial osteopathy, 116

diabetes, 89–90

diet, 30, 47–8

diet for basic health, 98–9

Do In, 118

Dolomite tablets, 62, 101

Eeman, L.E., 66

Eeman Technique, 66

electrocardiograph (EGC), 108

electroencephalographic
  readings (EEG), 59
environment, 41
enzymes, 108
exercise, 30, 69–70
  aerobic, 71
  isometric, 71
  isotonic, 71
  lack of, 20
  tolerance test, 27–8

familial
  hypercholesterolaemia,
  29, 82
family feuds, 43
fat intake, reduction
  of, 87–8
fats, polyunsaturated, 83,
  84, 87
  saturated, 83, 84
fatty deposits, 18
fibre, 95–6
fibrositis, 16
food preparation, 96–7
Friedman, Dr M., 37, 85

garlic tablets
  (capsules), 111
glyceryl trinitrate, 11, 72,
  108

Harvey, William, 15
heart attack, 17–18
heart, reconditioning
  of, 70–71
herbal preparations, 63
herbalism, medical, 111
herb teas, 61
hereditary factors, 29
Holmes, T.H., 39
homoeopathy, 112

Human Function
  Curve, 35–7, 43
human growth hormone
  (HGH), 59
hydrogenation, 87
hydrotherapy, 61
hyperventilation, 25

illness, purpose of, 42
indigestion, 16, 26
insomnia, 61
intercostal neuritis, 16
irisdiagnosis, 110
iron, 102

jogging, 73

kelp, 105

lecithin, 105
life-style audit, 46–7
lysine, 91

magnesium, 62, 100, 101
massage, 117–18
media-'hype', 32

naturopathic
  medicine, 110–11
noise, 41
noradrenalin, 20
nutrition, 62, 81–2

obesity, 20
occupational
  therapy, 53–4
osteopathy, 115
overcrowding, 115
oxygen, 20, 25

personality, 28
personality types, A, 37,
  38, 50, 107

B, 37-8
phosphorus, 101
platelets, sticky, 19
pollution, 41
potassium, 62, 93, 94, 101, 106
protein, 90-91
    first class, 91
pseudo angina, 16, 25, 28
pulse rate, 74

Qi gong, 75-6

Rahe, R.H., 39
reconditioning of the heart, 70-71
recreation, 58
reflex massages, 22
reflexology, 118
relaxation, 58, 64-6
relaxation routine, 67-9
responsibility, 43
rest, 58
restrictions of bones, 16
Rosenbaum, Dr R., 37, 85

salt, 94-5
Salutation to the Sun, 76, 77-9
Shiatzu, 118
siesta, 50, 63-4
sleep, benefits of, 58-60
sleep, rapid eye movement (REM), 60

smoking, 20
stress, 20, 34-5
sugar, 88-9
Swank, Dr R., 85
sunflower seeds, 92

tahini, 92
T'ai chi, 65, 75-6
Talbot, Dr G. Douglas, 84
targets, accessible, 49
tea, 61, 92
tofu, 92
training, 72
Treadmill of Effort, 38-9
tryptophan, 63

ventricles, 11, 17
viscero-somatic reflex, 26
vitamin B complex, 63, 100, 103
    B6, 100
    C, 100, 101, 104
    E, 101, 104

walking, 23, 73
warning signs, 43
wholefoods, 80, 97
work, planning of, 48-50
    pressures, 33, 48-9
    returning to, 55
working meals, 50-1

yoga, 75

zinc, 103